MG INTERNATIONAL

EDITED BY RICHARD L. KNUDSON

1977

CONTENTS

© Copyright, 1977
Richard L. Knudson
Published by MOTOR RACING PUBLICATIONS Ltd
56 Fitzjames Avenue, Croydon, Surrey, England
Made and printed in Great Britain by
The Garden City Press Limited
Letchworth, Hertfordshire SG6 1JS
ISBN 0 900549 35 1

INTRODUCTION

The preparation of this fourth annual publication has been an enjoyable task because it has brought me in contact with pleasant M.G. people from all over the world. It has also been especially interesting because of the new material about the marque which keeps appearing with amazing regularity. It convinces me that there is a wealth of material for subsequent annuals.

Regular readers will note the change in publishers, which means new approaches to marketing and a new title. The basic focus of the book remains the same as does the format. From the beginning I have tried to combine reports of meetings with a variety of historical and informative pieces. As promised, the emphasis will shift to the historical and away from reports on events. Club publications adequately cover the various meetings held around the world. This year I am introducing a "People and Places" feature which will be a photo section devoted to many recent meetings.

Two cars have been chosen as subjects for in-depth articles: the TC and the MGB. The TC has proudly carried the octagon for more than thirty years and did a great deal to insure the continued commercial success of our favourite marque. Introduced just after the close of World War II, the TC let the world know that the octagon spirit was alive and well in Abingdon. It was the TC which really started M.G. in the export business which has continued to the amazing success of the MGB. The tribute to the MGB is designed to give overdue recognition to the most successful sports car the world has ever known. I hope that this tribute will give impetus to the growing welcome of the MGB into the heart of the club movement on a world-wide basis. While the motoring press seems anxious to condemn the MGB as an antiquated design it continues to satisfy customers the world over. Why does it continue to please? If you bought this book, then you know why.

I have had an opportunity to savour the octagon spirit first hand this year by living in Abingdon. Oh, I know that 1976 isn't 1930, but that which Kimber started still survives. My family and I were made

to feel most welcome in Abingdon and all over England where we came in contact with many M.G. folk. The spirit which had its beginning in Oxford and Abingdon now circles the globe and has produced a unique enthusiast.

Living in Abingdon has afforded me an opportunity to meet many M.G. men from the past as well as the present. These people motivated me to put together the feature entitled "The Works Today", which gives some insight into what goes on at the factory in 1977. It is especially interesting that this follows immediately after the reproduction of that rare 1932 publication, *M.G. at the Sign of the Octagon*. Produced at a time when the company was trying to

establish itself as the world's largest and best manufacturer of sports cars, this interesting booklet describes more than a set of factory buildings—it lets the reader in on a way of life. If not written by Cecil Kimber, then it was certainly done under his direction.

The last page in this book is a somewhat sterile list of credits which I hope acknowledges all of the contributors of photographs and material. At the end of each article not written by me appears the name of the author. I want to take this opportunity to thank all of those contributors who have helped make this book for your enjoyment. Their enthusiasm for this annual has helped continue the project.

No, not the start of the Mille Miglia but a street scene in Vatra Dornei, a lovely old Rumanian town. The TD belongs to John Bekker of The Netherlands who logged 10,000 miles on his trip to the North Cape in Norway, through Finland, Russia and Rumania. His fascinating story begins on page 29 and is a true adventure.

I am always searching for new material and contributors. The M.G. story is far from being fully recorded, and this series of annuals will continue to be a voice to the continuing research being conducted by enthusiasts all over the world. If you have tracked down something of interest concerning a car, race, personality, or whatever that you think would interest a fellow M.G. enthusiast, then send it along to me at 21 Franklin Street, Oneonta, New York 13820, USA (all good things must end, and we will be back home after 1 August 1977). Even if you don't have an article or photos to contribute I would be interested in any suggestions you might have to make this series better.

Full recognition and gratitude go to the Leyland Photographic Department (John McLellan, John Cooper and John Harvey) and the newly created historical vehicles division who have been most co-operative and helpful in turning up some new and interesting photographs for our enjoyment. Leyland Historic Vehicles Limited is the official title given this new division, which has an immense task before it. This department is responsible for the historic vehicles and archives of the various marques which now make up the giant Leyland organization. The main vehicle display opened in September 1976 at Donington. The addition of the Leyland cars to Tom Wheatcroft's outstanding collection of single-seater racing cars makes the Donington museum a premier attraction for enthusiasts. An added attraction there will be the new racing circuit scheduled to open in the spring of 1977. It will be exciting to have a road course open once again at the site of England's first closed road course.

I think you will enjoy what follows in *M.G. International*. It has been created with Octagon Spirit and the true enthusiast in mind. You are obviously a true enthusiast of all things octagonal because you hold this book in your hands. And you have the Octagon Spirit; the combination of your spirit with that contained in this annual has kept the M.G. in the centre of sports car circles for over fifty years.

Dick Knudson

THE GANG DWINDLES

The 1935 M.G. racing mechanics at Brooklands; from left to right: Henry Stone, Bob Scott Reg (Jacko) Jackson and Alec Hounslow. Reg Jackson became the head of the department with Alec serving as his foreman. Henry Stone started with the competition department when the K3s were being prepared for the 1933 Mille Miglia. On the opposite page standing is Cecil Cousins; seated in the K3 is Alec Hounslow.

Although motor vehicles were made in the latter years of the nineteenth century, it needed World War I to provide the impetus for development, both of the vehicle itself and the means of production. Anyone who, having survived the 1914–18 war, entered the motor industry then, must now be at least as old as the century. It is not surprising, therefore, that those of us who have lived our lives with motor cars are now finding the names of our friends, in increasing numbers, in the obituary columns. It is distressing but it is an inescapable natural phenomenon.

Last year (1976) saw the death of three life-long stalwarts of the M.G. Car Company—Cecil Cousins, Reggie Jackson and Alec Hounslow. Having known each of them over a span of forty years or so, I could so easily write a book about each one of them and it is difficult to know how to do justice to the three of them in the confines of a page or so. Perhaps it will serve if I pick out one incident by which each of them sticks most firmly in my mind.

Cecil Cousins first imprinted himself on my mind about the middle of 1932, in the office of M.G.'s then Chief Engineer, H. N. Charles. As Service Manager at the time, I was discussing with "Charlie-Waggle" my daily crop of service complaints when the door opened, Cous came in staggering under a very heavy sack which he emptied in a heap on the office floor, delivering to Charles a tirade of quite unprintable

vituperative abuse. The first K chassis was in the design stage at the time and Cous had been to Goods Inwards to fetch the first set of chassis brackets which had just arrived. In his estimation they totalled somewhere near 150 lb and he thought Charles to be every kind of an idiot to design in so much dead weight—and said so in no uncertain terms. I escaped while the feathers were still flying but, of course, there was neither time nor money for steel forgings and Cous had been carrying bronze sand-castings.

Cecil, more than anyone I have ever known, had an M.G. fixation. He lived and breathed M.G. from the first time the name was ever thought of until he died. One could try to switch a conversation—to shoes, to ships, to sealing-wax—but in four sentences it would be back to M.G.—not just motor cars—M.G. He had no other interests outside his family, and I fancy he found his retirement very irksome in consequence.

Reggie Jackson, though every bit as staunch an M.G. devotee, by contrast had many outside interests. For years he gave much time and thought to local administration as a parish councillor, had a wide circle of friends, and used every minute of the day to be doing something, usually for somebody else.

From the earliest days he was a very good and ingenious mechanic and was a leading light in "Experi" and in the racing shop. He and Sydney Enever hunted as a pair and, with the cessation

of racing, the two of them became closely involved with the record-breaking forays and, even after Reggie had become M.G.'s Chief Inspector, still went out occasionally with the team.

A very vivid recollection of him dates from 1936 or thereabouts when a team of three M.G.s were running in a twelve-hour team race at Donington Park. Somehow or other I found myself as Team Manager of this operation and in charge of the M.G. pit. One of the cars came in on a non-scheduled stop and, as the hood was lifted, the carburettors burst into flames. I started shouting instructions, waving my arms and generally generating confusion and had reached a point where I had one man holding a fire-extinguisher pointed at the carbs and about to pull the trigger when a quiet, authoritative voice over my right shoulder said, "Put that thing down." That was all. The man lowered the extinguisher. Silence descended on the pit. And Reggie passed over an old sack—God knows how he came by it— and said, "Lay that over the carbs." This was done and the fire was out. What is more, the engine was still in a condition in which it could go.

Reggie had no position in the team. He was at Donington on a "busman's holiday" and just happened to be passing the pit at the critical time. In a flash, he took the situation in—me doing it all wrong—impending disaster—and stepped in with his superior experience and very quietly saved the day. It was a typical bit of Jackson which I shall never forget.

Alec Hounslow was in the thick of things from the earliest days and, all the time he was at Abingdon, was concerned with racing or experiment or prototype construction. He was a superlative fitter. The highlight of his earlier years was a riding mechanic to Nuvolari when they won the Tourist Trophy.

But, with the cessation of racing by M.G., Alec left Abingdon to find his fun elsewhere and worked on ERAs with various owners. With the outbreak of war, he joined the Royal Air Force and eventually found himself in Air-Sea Rescue. This, to Alec, was heaven—to be one of a small group with himself in charge of the engines was beyond his

dreams. On one occasion they rescued the crew of a Flying Fortress which had ditched in the North Sea "without them even getting their feet wet. They just walked down the wing and stepped straight into my ship." And, he adds: "That led to one of the wildest nights I can't remember."

On demobilization, back to Abingdon where, before long, he was in charge of a little shop that, in collaboration with Sydney Enever, carried on clandestine development work. (Design authority had been moved from Abingdon to Cowley, but everything was so slow and M.G. had such low priority that something had to be done.) Alec and his boys built HMO 6 and, later, they produced the prototype of the MGA.

I have hunted round for a photograph which I took of Alec on the Bonneville Salt Flats in Utah, in 1956 I think it was. Out there, with some forty of us—drivers, mechanics, timekeepers, crewmen—on the sun-baked salt twenty or so miles from human habitation, sanitation was, to say the least, primitive. A hole dug in the salt with a Charles Sale One-Holer perched over it was about as much as one could hope for. It was a beautiful picture against a cloudless blue sky, of Alec coming out! I'm sorry I can't find it. I feel sure that, as an epitaph, it would have appealed to his sense of humour.

John Thornley

The distinguished-looking group on the facing page (top) seem to be enjoying each other. The man on the extreme right is Reg Jackson. Reg is a hard man to find a photo of; next to him is Ken Wharton, then (r to l) we have Al Collinson, Dick Jacobs, Freddie Crossley, Syd Enever and Alec Hounslow. Between two M.G. milestones in the bottom picture stands Cecil Cousins who belongs there. The pleased-looking crew (above) have every right to be so, they have just completed EX182 for Le Mans. The man in the white coat in the middle is the affable Alec Hounslow.

MILESTONE
M.G.: THE TC

The Milestone Car Society is an international organization devoted to the recognition of those post-war automobiles which are deemed outstanding by the membership. Few thought that naming the TC one of the first nine Milestone Cars on the occasion of the formation of the organization in 1972 was anything more than inevitable. Though it was nominated on the strength of its design and performance, the Society's engineering and innovation criteria might equally have been applied. The reasons for selecting the TC as a charter Milestone were particularly solid. Aside from its vast qualifications as an automobile, it is one of the few vehicles to have inspired a whole

new way of looking at motorized transportation in the United States, though the concept was established long before in England. The TC's tangible and intangible qualities combined to make it one of the most successful sports cars ever built.

The TC was one of a long succession of M.G. Midgets which had its beginning with the M Type in 1929. Cecil Kimber, founder of The M.G. Car Company, realized that the public yearned for an affordable sports car. In the spring of 1928 Morris Motors was planning a "baby car" with a potent Wolseley engine, to be called the Morris Minor. Kimber took the Minor chassis and fitted a special two-seater

body shell supplied by Carbodies of Coventry; he had created his first cheap and cheerful Midget—the M Type. It was shown on the company's stand at the 1928 Motor Show, but it was not until March 1929 that the first production M Types were completed at the assembly facility located on Edmund Road in Oxford.

The M Type proved to be so popular that it soon became necessary to find a larger factory. Late in 1929 the company moved to its present location in Abingdon, a few miles from Oxford, and the production of the M Type continued. It is to Kimber's credit that he, and subsequently the company, never lost sight of the original premise: an enjoyable sports car within the reach of the working man. Henry Ford had proved the validity of the concept with his passenger car and put many Americans behind the wheel. Without M.G. many people would never have experienced the joys of owning and driving a sports car. Right through to the present Midget being assembled at Abingdon, there has always been an effort to provide a maximum amount of performance and enjoyment into a reasonably priced machine. Predictably, M.G. has been the world's largest producer of sports cars since the 1930's.

It is to the J2, introduced in 1932 to replace the M Type, that the TC owes most of its styling characteristics. This successful model was the first of the stylized Midgets with the appearance that would say "M.G." and "Sports Car" to the world for at least twenty-five years. The familiar radiator grille was right out front and was retained from previous models. For the first time on a production car appeared the double-humped cowl and cutaway doors. The J2 designers also replaced the M Type's boat-tail with the now familiar slab petrol tank and rear-mounted spare tyre. It was not until 1933, however, that the cycle fenders were replaced by swept clamshell fenders which were delicate and pleasing to the eye.

The TA Midget appeared in 1936 with several features which would enhance the TC in 1945. The basic shape, of course, was established, but the body of the TA was enlarged a great deal. The bigger body was made possible by the larger chassis. The major technical difference was the use of a pushrod engine instead of the popular overhead-cam power plant. Enthusiasts lamented the demise of the ohc engine, but the company had decided that the problems of keeping it going properly could be solved by using an engine which theoretically would not require such careful attention. The TA engine was the Wolseley Ten or, more properly, the Morris Ten, and it was designated the MPJG. It displaced 1292 cc and produced 52.4 bhp at 5000 rpm. The TA did not cost any more than the previous PB, and as soon as purists recovered

from the loss of the smaller, saucier P Type, it was readily welcomed.

One might think that since the TA is such a close relative of the TC, pinpointing its designer would be a simple thing. History is always difficult because it is written after the fact; while it is happening, little record is kept because it does not seem particularly important at the time. Before his death in February 1976, I had the opportunity to discuss this matter with Cecil Cousins. Cousins was the very first employee of The M.G. Car Company and rose through the ranks to become works director by the time of his retirement in 1967.

"Abingdon had its own drawing office until June of 1935," said Cousins, "when we were bought off of, I suppose, Lord Nuffield. Or was he Sir William Morris? I don't know, it doesn't matter anyway—same bloke. He sold us hook, line and sinker to Morris Motors. Up until then it had been a private company owned by Sir William Morris. Well, as soon as Morris Motors got hold of us they shut down our drawing office and said to stop all of this nonsense of racing and record-breaking and make some money. All of our drawing office boys went to Cowley." Cowley was the Morris Motors headquarters on the outskirts of Oxford. Wilson McComb's book, *Story of the M.G. Sports Car*, tells us that H. N. Charles, the long-time chief designer, made the move but that Syd Enever and Bill Renwick stayed at Abingdon as design liaison men.

"The first car to come out of the Morris Motors' drawing office," Cousins continues, "was the two litre SA, which was a modified eighteen-horse Morris. The first Midget was the TA."

When asked if the TA was a team effort, he responded: "You have to remember that Cowley wasn't far from Abingdon. Kimber kept popping in and popping out saying, 'I don't like this, and I don't like that, and I don't like the other.' There was a certain amount of back pressure from Abingdon all the time so that they didn't get too far off the beaten track. The TA was, in fact, the first Midget designed by the new alternative drawing office. That was

all right as we used the existing ten-horse Morris engine in that car. You see, in those days, we didn't sell engines by cubic capacity. We built engines on a cranky thing called the RAC rating, which didn't take into consideration the cubic capacity of the engine. It was based, pure and simple, on the bore of the engine; hence the fact that for years and donkey's years, all the English motor trade suffered with great engines with tiny little bores and whacking great, long strokes." It is, then, difficult to exactly pinpoint the TA's designer. It was probably largely H. N. Charles's work with Syd Enever leading the Abingdon input. Kimber was unquestionably the boss and ultimately responsible. In fact, the TA was the only T Series Midget which received real Kimber input—but if the TA, then certainly the TC (which appeared after his death) was a product of his imagination.

The next Midget was the TB, merely a TA with a new engine, appearing in September 1939. Only 379 were built before the factory's World War II work caused sports car production to cease. It is interesting to note, however, that as late as April 1940 there still was a corner of the factory devoted to production. The TB engine was the famous XPAG unit used on the later TC, Y, TD, and TF. Displacement dropped from the 1292 cc of the TA to 1250 cc; dimensions changed from 63.5 × 102 mm bore and stroke to 66.5 × 90 mm. The end result was a most dependable engine which not only powered many sports cars from Abingdon but also a wide variety of racing and record-breaking cars as well.

As the country became more and more involved in the war all car production at Abingdon ceased, and M.G. men who did not go to war were busy in a variety of defence projects. These included everything from tank repair to the assembly of a major aircraft component. Kimber left M.G. during this period and was killed in a train accident in February 1945, a few months before the factory resumed sports car production.

"Kimber had left and was dead," Cecil Cousins continued. "We had a new managing director, a very clever businessman by the name of H. A. Ryder. He had been director of the Morris Radiator Company, a very clever engineer, but he'd never made a motor car nor had anything to do with anybody who had. He was a wonderful sheet metal man—the champion sheet metal worker of the Midlands in his earlier days. After the war we said, 'What will we make?' He said, 'Well, we'd better make the TB again.' Luckily, somebody wisely added, 'Well, we'd better find out what was wrong with it.'

"So they went through the records to find out what items we had the biggest numbers of service complaints on and that sort of public criticism. The only two things that anybody could point to was that it wasn't wide enough and that the sliding shackles were the biggest service item. So, they made the body four inches wider across the cockpit and replaced the sliding trunnions with rubber-mounted shackles to get over the other problem. And that was how the TC came to be. We announced it in October 1945 and had built eighty-one by the end of the year."

The British motoring press was enthusiastic in its welcome of the TC. Road tests appeared in *The Motor* (10 October 1945) and *The Autocar* (12 October 1945)—both praised it highly. The latter's Montague Tombs reported "a dashing sort of performance, smartness off the mark and quick acceleration". He concluded that "the little car is rock steady and stable, and handles with a satisfying accuracy. It is quite charming to drive fast . . . in short, the car is an extremely well-balanced design."

Tombs also summarized the improvements and modifications from the TB. In addition to the two major differences previously mentioned, he noted new Luvax-Girling shock absorbers, a single 12 V battery mounted in the firewall, a large toolbox behind the battery box, new instruments and a fuel reserve warning light. Under the bonnet, appearance was improved with wires and pipes neatly grouped; the engine was finished in grey instead of black, though the grey later gave way to M.G. Maroon. In production, Tombs reported that cars would be done in

Above is a bench used for the assembly of the front axle of the TC. This is the sort of final assembly of components which still takes place at Abingdon. On the opposite page we see a rolling chassis ready for the engine installation. Restorers should find some useful details in the close study of photographs such as these.

black with a choice of red, green or biscuit trim; black, then, was the only colour available for the 1945 TC. Later colour options included: M.G. Red, Regency Red, Shires Green, Almond Green, Ivory, Clipper Blue, as well as black. Wheels were painted silver and radiator slats usually matched the interior colour.

The Motor's test was more factual and was based on stopwatch figures and factory specifications. Even their writers were impressed, and they let the public know about it: "A high performance small car, one that will doubtless give great pleasure to a large number of sporting motorists." They further praised the high mechanical efficiency of the

XPAG engine: "The comparatively high specific output has not been obtained at the expense of low-end torque. On the contrary, the power curve reveals a bmep in excess of 100 lb at 1000 rpm and over 120 lb between 1700 rpm and 4200 rpm. These figures have been secured not only by careful porting and camshaft design, but also by maintaining a better than usual mechanical efficiency over a wide speed range. The figure on this count reaches 90 per cent at 800 rpm, and is held to 80 per cent at 4000 rpm, which is the equivalent of 2350 ft per minute piston speed." Further, "It is therefore reasonable to suppose that this car is fully capable of sustained cruising speeds of 65–70

mph, where road conditions permit, without overstressing the engine."

Coupling this 1250 cc, 54.4 bhp engine to the rear wheels was a marvellous gearbox—special builders until recently have sought the TC transmission to handle racing chores in cars of up to 100 bhp. The final ratios were: first, 17.32; second, 10.00; third, 6.93; top, 5.125. The gearbox is nicely located and a delight to use; synchromesh is available on the top three gears. The normal rear axle ratio is 5.125:1, giving a speed of 15.84 mph per 1000 rpm in top gear.

Aesthetically speaking, the TC is beautiful. Most striking are the big, bold radiator and the long bonnet

13

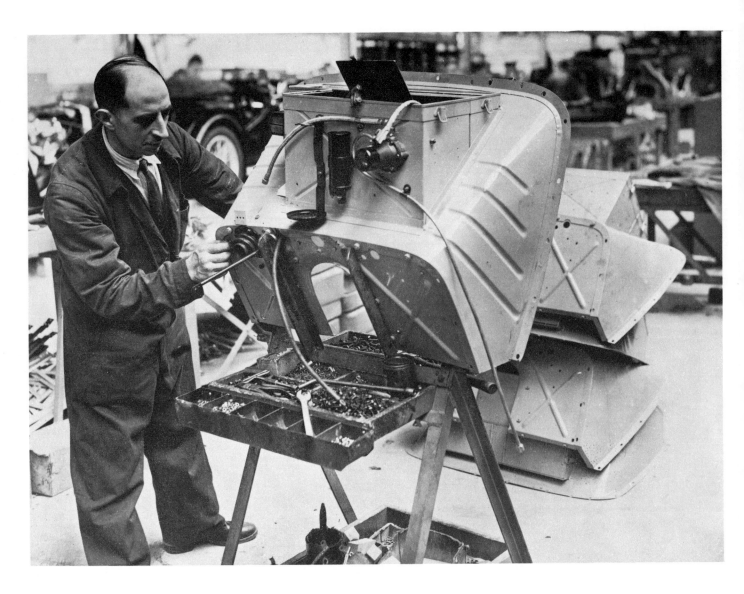

leading to it; next, one's eyes are attracted to the delicate clamshell fenders framing spidery, 19 in. wheels. It's truly the picture of a classic sports car. The coachwork is in proper proportion to the chassis dimensions. Even with the windscreen erected and all of the weather equipment in place, the automobile looks correct. John Thornley called the K3 the epitome of the M.G., I agree with his evaluation for the racing models, but among the sports cars, the TC comes as near to being the epitome as any. A TC was one of eight automobiles chosen for the New York Museum of Modern Art exhibit devoted to classic design in 1951. There is no question that the TC is an almost

perfect combination of vintage beauty and modern performance.

Today, as ever, there is endless discussion about what makes a classic—especially among automobile enthusiasts. Whenever the talk centres on sports cars, the TC is always included. The July 1975 issue of *Road & Track* had a feature article about a special show devoted to the auto as an art form. That show sought to choose cars which were outstanding combinations of the aesthetic art of the body designer and the technical innovations of the mechanical engineer. The main purpose of the show was a focus on the automobile as a visual art form as it developed since its inception. The

This period photo should also settle some arguments. The placement of the fuel lines is exact. The most interesting item, however, is the oil can holder. How many TCs today have one fitted? The completed chassis (opposite, top) is ready for a body. In the bottom photo are cars at the end of the assembly line ready for testing.

oldest car in the show was a 1903 Autocar; the newest was a 1975 Scirocco. In between were fifty-eight cars which represented a wide variety of marques, most of which would be readily accepted at any *concours* in the world. One of the first post-war cars at the show was a 1948 TC. The judges offered the following reasons for including it: "Things come together with honesty, clarity, delicacy. The overall balance from any view is so digestable and believable. The major impact: fun, excitement, affordability ... a classical statement of 'dignity' in its smallest automotive form ... Abingdon's pride won world popularity with its meticulously formed fenders, geometric hood, and neat body." These words from the highly respected Harry Bradley, Tom Kellogg and Strother MacMinn appeared in the show's lovely catalogue and certainly summarize the feelings knowledgeable enthusiasts have for this delightful sports car from the banks of the Thames.

That the TC was America's introduction to popular sports cars is an indisputable fact. True, sports cars and road racing existed in the USA prior to World War II, but only for a very few exceptional men who were members of the Automobile Racing Club of America. The average American enthusiast, however, was not economically able to think about owning a sports car until after the war. When the war ended England was flooded with American soldiers, and they were introduced to a variety of sports cars which gave amazing performance on twisting country lanes. Many of these cars were M.G.s. Given the basic American love of the automobile, it should come as no surprise that many G.I.s brought M.G.s back when they returned from the war.

When these first cars hit the American streets, interest increased. It must be pointed out that a dealer network was not immediately available. Importation of TCs was not an overnight event, nor did TCs go to the States in huge amounts. There were sufficient numbers of TCs to start the sports car revolution which really spread after the introduction of the TD, but American sales did

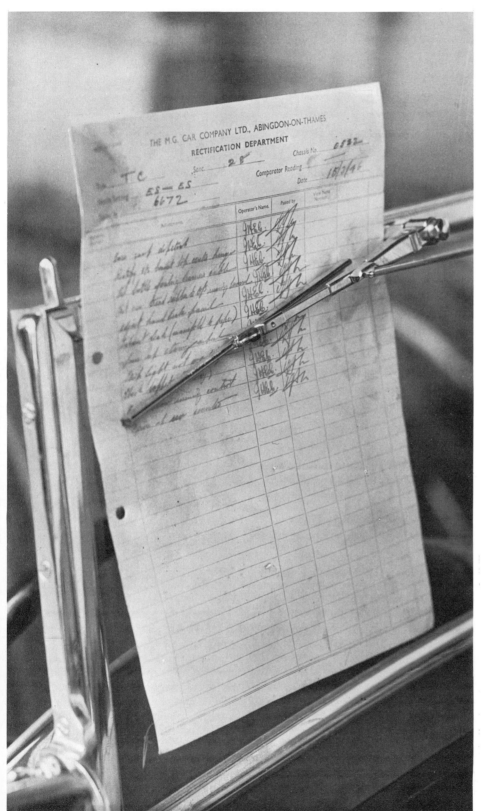

not account for a majority of the production run as is sometimes believed.

A look at the production figures at this point would help explain the number of cars which actually went to America.

TC PRODUCTION AND EXPORT

	Chassis		
Year	from	To	Total
1945	0251	0329	78
1946	0330	1994	1665
1947	1995	4248	2254
1948	4249	7415	3167
1949	7416	10,251	2836
Grand total			10,000
Total British sales			3408
Total overseas sales			6592
Total USA sales			2001

NOTE: The factory parts book (AKD 856) specifies that USA export models started at chassis number 7380.

The original American importer was Motor Sport, Inc. of New York, owned by Sam and Miles Collier. These men were in business before the war and had been active in the ARCA. Their major business interests were not in cars, so they gave way to a larger national sales network which developed. Prominent on the East Coast was J. S. Inskip, Inc., which took over from Motor Sport, Inc. just prior to the 1948 New York Auto Show. On the West Coast Kjell Qvale had started his British Motor Car

The owner of TC 0522 should be happy to see this photo. This is an example of the close inspection each car received upon completion. The same practice exists today. On the opposite page are views of both sides of the popular XPAG powerplant.

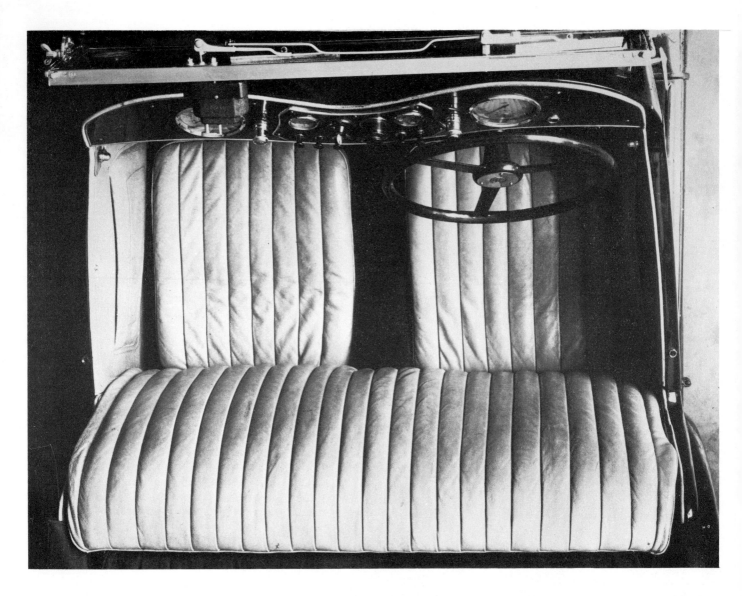

Distributors in 1947. Qvale had seen the TC while in the service and realized its sales potential in his part of the country. In 1948 he sold seventy-five cars, and from that beginning has grown a dealer network of over 100 outlets. The Hambro Trading Company of America, Inc. became the sole concessionaires in America for the Nuffield organization during the late 1940's. Early in 1950 they listed the following distributors: British Motor Car Company, San Francisco; International Motors, Inc., Los Angeles; J. S. Inskip, Inc., New York; S. H. Lynch, Dallas; and Waco Motors, Miami.

Since the TC did not arrive in any great numbers, it is not surprising that mention of it in American magazines was slow in coming. The late Tom McCahill was the first to test it. Indeed, McCahill was the first to test most cars, especially foreign cars, in American magazines, and his work usually appeared in *Mechanix Illustrated*. His TC test in the January 1949 issue showed he loved it. Describing an impromptu dice between his Mercury and a TC, McCahill recounted that he could beat the TC on a straightaway or long steep hill, but '...the rest of the time, he made me feel like an idiot. He was so agile.., on winding portions of the road he drove me crazy. He could take a flat, hard curve at 75 and not lean as much as two degrees while I was pulling every trick in the book to keep from rolling over."

Owning a sports car in those early days presented certain problems to American enthusiasts. While some dealers were excellent, others were marginal at best—hmmm, maybe things haven't changed all that much. The sports car required careful tuning and regular maintenance; if the owner could not do it himself, then he was in trouble. The M.G. was known, however, for running *forever* once it was in tune. When asked if M.G.s weren't fussy beasts, Cecil Cousins retorted, "Why not compare a knife to an axe. They both cut. If you want to cut something, you can take a heavy axe and if you hit the thing

enough you'll wear through. With a good knife, however, you want to cherish and hone and oil it until it's at the point where it will do exactly what you want of it. That's the way it is with an M.G.''

It is always interesting to consider the famous people who owned and therefore sanctioned a particular car, and a popular notion has it that famous people have good taste. It has been said that the first TC went to the Sheriff of Nottingham; one assumes that it did not see much service on the trails of Sherwood Forest. We know that Prince Philip owned one, so in this Silver Jubilee Year for Queen Elizabeth we can claim some M.G. one-upmanship—

she was courted in a TC. Ernest Hemingway and John O'Hara were two American men of letters who enjoyed the TC. Several Hollywood types owned them, but we can't be too sure of their reasoning.

It is impossible to determine the number of world calibre drivers who had their first experiences in a TC, but there were many. Phil Hill, Carroll Shelby, Richie Ginther and John Fitch were Americans who drove them. In England George Phillips, Ted Lund and Dick Jacobs were driving works-prepared TCs in a variety of races. Phillips went on to drive a special-bodied TC in the 1949 and 1950 Le Mans races; in 1950 he finished second in class.

This unusual view of the interior (opposite) supplies ample detail. With everything so close at hand it is little wonder that the TC continues to delight owners everywhere Full weather protection (above) was the claim for the TC's hood and side screens. It made a snug, comfortable cockpit even if those twin rear windows did hinder visibility quite a bit.

While dependable performance is what established the TC as a respected sports car during its production years, its classic beauty is the quality which makes it one of the most desired Milestone cars today. The TC has everything that says "M.G." to the world as it embodies the best design elements from every Midget which preceded it. The square radiator, long bonnet, cutaway doors, and big wire wheels all combine in a classic look that will always appeal to sports car enthusiasts everywhere they gather.

A conservative estimate is that a quarter of the 10,000 TCs produced survive today. Those left, barring natural disasters, should never be destroyed.

And it appears that very few now change hands. Not so long ago major magazines and papers always listed some TCs for sale; today, it is rare if one appears. Occasionally one will be seen on one of the numerous auction blocks that beseige the hobby today; happily, that, too, is a rare happening. Neither do we hear of parts cars being broken up as the prevailing attitude is that *anything* can be restored. As a result enthusiasts are starting from junk chassis and gradually building complete cars. And this can be done as there are sources for remanufactured parts and technical help and encouragement.

Owning a restored TC does not imply making a museum piece out of it. The

car is not a bit more fragile today than when it was introduced in 1945. It can easily keep up with modern traffic; one can be confident that if anything goes wrong it is repairable. Driving a TC is as enjoyable today as it always has been. People admire it for what it is. Those admiring looks, waves and comments are ample rewards for the hours spent in careful restoration, but the real pleasure comes from driving it over a piece of challenging country road.

So that is the story of the Milestone TC. Why was it made a Milestone? Well, to quote Louis Armstrong's reply when someone asked him to rationalize jazz, "If you got to ask why, you ain't ever going to know."

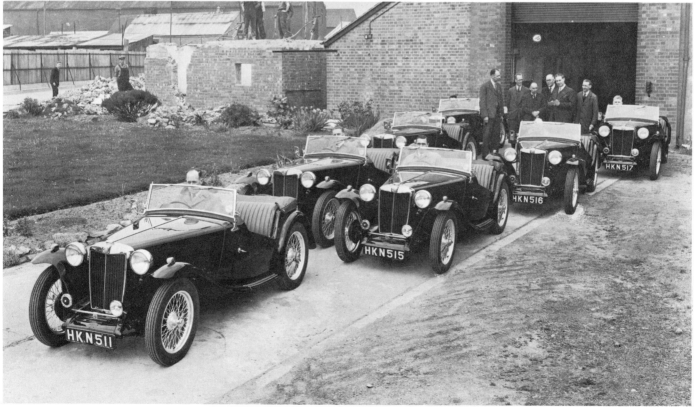

While the above photo might have easily been taken in 1948 it is actually very recent. Bred on competition, the TC still thrives on it. On the previous page (top) is a TC being road-tested wearing a temporary works plate, and in the bottom picture we see a group of TCs being delivered at the works. On the opposite page we have two TCs prepared for M.G. Car Club racing.

24

On these two pages are scenes
of another type of competition to reward
the careful restorer. Many organizations have
judged meets while others rely on a
popular vote to determine winning cars.
Above we see a happy owner at Beaulieu
being presented his trophy by Captain Eyston.
Opposite (top) is a line-up of TCs at the
Eagle Bay Gathering of the Faithful sponsored
by The New England M.G.T Register. The
bottom photograph shows more lovely TCs
at the New Hope Show held each August in
Pennsylvania.

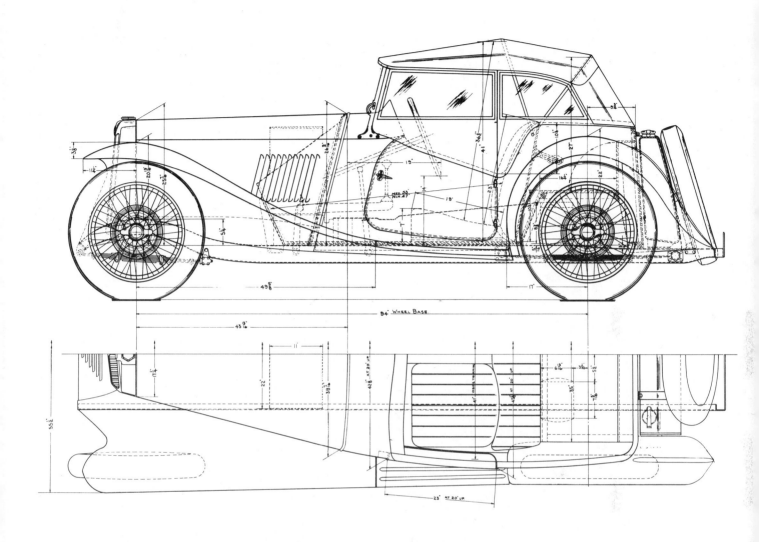

94" WHEEL BASE.

Maintaining the Breed

Bred true to type, the MG Midget T.C. Series possesses all the stamina and resilience of its predecessors. Chief among its many virtues are lively acceleration, lightning response to controls, superb braking power and inherent roadworthiness.

Price £412.10.0 ex works plus Purchase Tax £115.6.8.

Safety Fast!

TO RUSSIA WITH TD: A MODERN ADVENTURE

Johnny Bekker is a well-known M.G. enthusiast, and his TD is seen in many faraway places. He long dreamed of an extended trip in his M.G. behind the Iron Curtain. It is exactly the sort of adventure which many of us dream about but never, for a variety of reasons, seem able to bring to reality. Johnny did it, and his recounting of the adventure he found with his TD in the summer of 1976 is both a pleasure and a challenge to all of us who dream about doing similar things in an M.G.

The months before my 11 June 1976 departure had been busy. Getting ready for a 10,000-mile trip in a TD takes time: spraying the car M.G. Red, rebuilding the engine, collecting spares, and making last-minute adjustments. This was to be the trip of a lifetime, and I wanted to be ready for it in every way.

My first stop from The Hague was scheduled for Oslo where John Erik Skjefstad was awaiting me. The trip through The Netherlands, Germany and Denmark was an easy one, and I averaged 50 mph. Because I was anxious to reach Oslo, I did not stop in Denmark, but headed straight for the Frederikshavn—Goteborg ferry. The boat was loaded with young Swedes who were making a round trip on the ferry because they could buy unlimited alcohol on board. The customs man asked me why I hadn't purchased any spirits on the boat, and was surprised to learn that their tax-free prices were higher than shop prices in Holland. Petrol, however, was about 20 per cent cheaper in Sweden, so not everything is expensive in that country.

At 2.30 am, with the sun almost coming up, the ferry docked, and I took to the road again. Since I was sleepy, I stopped a couple of times for a nap; as a result, I did not arrive in Oslo until 7.30 am. The journey from The Hague took me an hour and a half longer than John Erik Skjefstad's record of twenty-four hours for the Oslo—Amsterdam trip.

I enjoyed my brief visit with John Erik, who was delighted to show me around Oslo. The next day I headed for the fjord country. I left the main road in Fagernes for the crossing of the Jotunheimen Mountains, then I followed the Otta River to the west. I had planned to visit Geiranger, one of the most scenic parts of the fjord country, but the roads were still full of snow so that I had to make a 100-mile detour to rejoin my planned route. Then it was a fast drive to Trondheim through some marvellous countryside. I was surprised to see how many differences there were: one minute between snow walls, then beside green meadows with cows; sometimes in the clouds, then, after some ser-pentine curves, dropping out of the clouds into the sun again. There were views which rivalled the Swiss Alps. It was 9.00 pm when I arrived in Trondheim where I visited Halvor Westgaard. Halvor uses his F Type daily, and we made a tour of the city in it at midnight when it was still light enough to read.

From Trondheim I drove quickly north, making 300 miles every day. I passed through Steinkjer, Bodo, Narvik and Tromso. Tromso is situated on a small island, and is a nice town. Most of it is built from wood; its cathedral is one of the largest wooden buildings in Norway. Although Tromso is well above the Arctic Circle, it is not cold. Temperatures seldom drop below —15°C, while in the summer it can be as warm as 25°C, thanks to the Gulf Stream.

From this point it was a short distance to the North Cape. In Olderfjord one leaves the E6 to cover the last miles to Repvag, where one must take the ferry to the island of Mageroy on which is located the North Cape. I arrived at noon in very nice weather. The first thing I encountered was a parking lot where I was charged a fee to park, Behind the lot is a heated restaurant; thereafter, it is a short walk to the fence behind which is an endless view of the Arctic Ocean. Since there is no road for these last few feet, cars are not permitted to actually go to this northernmost point. I thought it madness to have

come so far in the TD then not be able to take it to the very tip, so I spoke some friendly words to the parking attendant, and was able to do it.

Although quite windy, the sun was shining and it wasn't cold. Two hours later, however, the clouds came in, reducing visibility to 50 or 60 ft. I had hoped to take some photos at midnight, but the clouds prevented that. I was pleased that they had stayed away when I arrived so that I was able to take some pictures at this famous spot.

Looking back on the trip to the Cape through Norway, I couldn't have been more pleased with the start to my adventure. The landscape is varied indeed: lovely hills, high mountains,

roads along the fjords, over passes, going on, sometimes, for countless miles through the tundra where only the surface of the ground ever defrosts in the summer, so that the water can never sink into the ground. At times I would not see a house for hours; far up north I encountered the Laps, who surprised me a bit with their commercial efforts at selling souvenirs from tents alongside the road. From halfway up in Norway the sun stays up day and night; at midnight the countryside becomes eerie— a remote place, but interesting.

From the North Cape it was a short journey to Finland then down to Helsinki in the space of three days. The Finnish landscape is not so interesting

This last stretch of desolate road straight through the tundra-like landscape of northernmost Norway is as spectacular as it is lonely. On the opposite page John Bekker's TD is dwarfed between walls of snow in the fjord country near Geiranger.

as the Norwegian; it consists mainly of flat country, a few hills, many lakes, and large forests. In Lapland, one has to be wary of the swarms of mosquitoes; I was lucky not to be bothered by them—the few which were present could be easily discouraged with the help of a big Dutch cigar. After Helsinki, it was on to Russia.

Some of you might have the idea that travelling on your own in the USSR is complicated, if not impossible. There were some things which had to be taken care of early, but it was not all that difficult. First of all, one can only stay in about thirty different towns and not all of these having camping sites; these towns are interconnected with specific roads on which you must travel. After obtaining an Intourist (the Russian State Travel Agency) map, I picked my route through Russia: Leningrad, Novgorod, Kalinin, Moscow, Oryol, Kiev, Vinnitsa, Chernovtsy and Kishinev. Next it was to a travel office connected with Intourist; they booked the trip through the head office in Moscow. I was sent a confirmation and a bill for all of my lodgings. After the bill was paid, the Russian Embassy issued me a visa without any fuss. The visa is a separate document which is not attached to the passport. Although the issuing of the visa only took a couple of days, the whole process I just described can take as long as four months. One really should start well in advance. Further, plan your route well because it is not always easy to change once inside Russian borders.

After passing the Finnish border, I came immediately to a small Russian post. The two soldiers there studied my passport, made a few notes and a telephone call, and then sent me on my way. I was congratulating myself on how easy it had all been when two miles further on I came to the real customs house, a giant building with many officials. Most of the traffic there consisted of large tourist buses. All of the passengers had to exit with their luggage while the bus drove over a pit so the officers could look under, in and through the bus.

These buses caused individual cars such as mine a considerable wait. Finally, an official took my passport and returned thirty minutes later with my travel programme. Shortly after a crew arrived to search the TD. The man in charge spoke English and looked in all the bags, under the car, under the bonnet, poked with a wire in the petrol tank, and asked if I had any literature with me. I had to declare money and jewellery. At all times he was, like all Russian officials I met, very polite and friendly. After another short wait my passport was returned, and I received permission to leave the control.

Traffic rules in Russia are the same as all over Europe. Roads are not always

first class, but on the average they are quite good; newly built highways are excellent, but all are two lanes only. I did not see any motorways. Traffic can be quite heavy. Outside of towns it consists mainly of trucks and buses running on 72 (indeed, 72) octane petrol. Fortunately, most of the new cars they build (mainly the Lada) require 95 octane so the TD did not suffer. I found petrol quite reasonable; it cost a third of what it sells for in Holland. I had to buy special coupons with Western money. Later on I discovered that not all petrol stations accept the coupons, but that it was possible to buy it at the discounted price.

Interest in the M.G. was very high,

On both pages here are views of picturesque Tromso, a lovely fishing community located on a small island in northern Norway. The island is joined to the mainland by a modern bridge. There are many interesting wooden buildings, and the waterfront is always active with fishing boats coming and going.

The TD is as far north as it can go without getting wet. Behind the fence at the North Cape the land drops straight into the Arctic Ocean. This point is situated at the same latitude as Cape Barrow in Alaska. On the opposite page the TD is parked in front of the Winter Palace in Leningrad where the Czars used to live. Completed in 1762, it now houses a famous art collection.

especially during the petrol stops. You see, in Russia there are only Russian-made cars. Every tourist car, then, is a curiosity, but an open red TD was a real rarity. Russian truck drivers, who have to be good mechanics as well, were especially interested when I opened the bonnet. They would ask: *skoljko kilomjetrov* (how many kilo-metres), *benzina ili dizil* (gasoline or diesel), *dwa karbjuratori* (two carburet-tors), and so on; as you will notice, many technical words are just about the same. Written in their own alphabet, these words look like abracadabra, but once one learns their alphabet it clears up. When speaking with Russians, they often will understand some English

words and you their Russian. When communication becomes difficult, one can always use the hand or foot or draw pictures.

There were many policemen on the roads and in the cities. All traffic between cities is only possible with a permit, and they have checkpoints to keep an eye on the traffic. Now the speed limit outside of town is 56 mph, but you must slow to 25 mph when going by a checkpoint. Over that, and you'll be stopped. I was stopped twice without penalty, but they made their point quite clear by pointing to the speedometer. I was stopped another two times for having taken the wrong road accidentally, after which I was

nicely put on the right course. Sometimes we get the impression that they are being oppressive with all of their police, but it may not be all that different from the West where traffic police keep a watchful eye.

The countryside is not interesting in Russia because it is so flat. Often one passes through little villages which have only dirt side roads because the local transport is by horse and cart; with these the people carry products from the fields to the shops. They are never in a hurry. Wood is used for construction with some buildings being very old. Here and there one sees a little church with typical onion top. Most village churches create a neglected impression in contrast to some of those in cities.

I enjoyed the cities because I was free to go where I wished, and there were many interesting things to see. Leningrad was very nice for historical and contemporary reasons. It was founded by Tsar Peter the Great around 1700, and was built according to a plan. All of the monumental buildings are in the same style. It is a handsome city comparable to Paris.

Moscow, on the other hand, has a totally different character: the roads leading to the centre are often very wide; traffic can be quite heavy, but they really don't know what big city rush-hours are like. One sees many skyscrapers, not unlike Chicago, dating from the thirties as well as new buildings. The focal point of Moscow is the Kremlin and its surroundings. The Kremlin is a big fortress with towers and walls. Inside one finds old cathedrals (now museums) and the governmental buildings. The places around the Kremlin are always busy with people; most of them are Russian tourists, but many foreigners are in Moscow as well. One can buy snacks and ice cream; there are lotteries, book shops, souvenir shops—actually not much different from other big cities we know. The choice in the shops seemed adequate but there were no articles from the West to be seen. Quality might have been down but so were the prices.

When travelling through Russia, the prepaid lodging includes the free use of an Intourist guide for three hours a day. In the big cities this usually means a bus tour. In the smaller places the guide usually accompanies you in your own car which makes the tour much more interesting, especially because these guides often are young ladies. Most are students who speak a variety of languages. In this situation I was a popular tourist—I wonder if it was my car? We talked not only of the historical points of interest, but also about other subjects as well. I regularly asked if they were at all interested in visiting other countries. The answer was always in the negative and probably motivated by two reasons: 1—it is difficult to obtain permission to travel outside Russia, and 2—costs of such a trip would be excessive.

Camping in the USSR was not what I was used to: there were few hot showers, toilets were often dirty, and a general lack of up-keep. In years to come, such things will improve.

In reflection, I feel that the Russian people don't have the freedom of mobility which we enjoy nor can they speak freely. They do not have the opportunity to obtain information via the press about the West the way we are able to learn about them.

I left the Soviet Union through Leusheny, which brought me into Rumania. Although this, too, was a communist country, what a contrast it

This is the other side of the palace square in Leningrad. In the background is the arch of the former General Staff Building; on top of the arch is a chariot of Victory. This may well be the only TD to be photographed in this spot.

provided to Russia. On one side of the border are the Russians with their tidy, green uniforms, their big customs buildings, and their bureaucracy which cost me two hours to get out of the country. On the other side are the Rumanians with slipshod, brown uniforms, a little building with four people present who needed only ten minutes to get me through. For Rumania one needs a visa which I obtained on entry for a modest fee. Further, I had to change in advance the equivalent of $10 for each day I planned to stay; this money could not be taken out of the country. I needed it for petrol, which I found to be as expensive as at home.

Rumania is nice; you can go where you like and stay where you like. It is beautiful, with plains, rolling hills and high mountains, as can be seen by the old castles, fortresses and fortified towns. I stopped to buy some food in Vatra Dornei, and when I returned to the TD it was hidden completely from sight by a mob of people. This happened more than once in Rumania where foreign cars are seldom seen. The car most popular here is the Dacia, the Rumanian version of the Renault 12.

From Vatra Dornei I went over the Borgo Pass to Bistrita. This pass is often cited as the place where Count Dracula lived; his castle, however, is not to be found here, but elsewhere as we shall see later on. From Bistrita I went to Sibiu via Alba Iulia. I spent a Sunday there; the many people walking

*An equally rare place
for M.G.s is in front of the
Cathedral of St. Basil the Blessed. Built
in 1555–1560, it is a gem of old
Russian architecture. At the other
side of the cathedral, which is
now a museum, one
finds the famous Red Square.*

the streets certainly enjoyed seeing the TD from Holland.

The next day was an exciting one which brought both highlights and disaster. From Sibiu I headed across the Fagaras Mountains. The road was quite new but unsurfaced; as a result, I had to hold my speed under 20 mph. The road took me high into the mountains; since it was a cloudy day, the visibility was limited. On top I drove through a short tunnel which had potholes 3 ft deep and water pouring from the walls like minature waterfalls. The tunnel was completely full of clouds so that I had to use extreme care finding my way through—I was actually afraid of becoming lost in a tunnel. I came through safely and enjoyed the descent leading to Lake Vidraru. As soon as I had passed the lake, the road became excellent and took me along the banks of the Arges River into the Wallachian Plain. Here I found the real castle of Dracula. It was built by Vlad the Impaler (Vlad Tepes) who earned his name by disposing of his enemies by skewering them on a long stake; sometimes he slaughtered whole cities this way. He lived from 1431 until 1476 and was the son of Vlad Dracul, a name which means devil as well as dragon. His son, Vlad Tepes, acquired the nickname of Dracula which actually means son of Dracul. And there you are, the real Dracula, who was as bloodthirsty with his impaling as was his fiction counterpart. A long set of steps leads up to the castle ruin. When I was up there the sun was shining, and I felt very well; other people, however, seem to have accidents or become ill shortly afterwards. Of course, I don't believe in such things, but about three hours after I left the castle, the TD's gearbox packed up and the M.G. was out of action for the next eight days.

The cause of the breakdown was a bearing failure. The trouble came about ten miles away from the small village of Cimpulung. A friendly Rumanian who spoke a little French guided me to the town and invited me to stay at his home. After tearing the gearbox down with some local help, I realized that I needed parts, so I took a train to Bucharest, 100 miles away. From Bucharest I

called Holland and arranged what I needed. The Dutch Automobile Club picked up my spare gearbox, took it to Schipol Airport, and sent it to me. The costs of this, by the way, were taken care of by the Dutch Automobile Club to which I pay a modest annual fee. The gearbox arrived on a Friday afternoon, but I could not pick it up at that time because the customs office closed at noon. The next day I went back with a man from the auto club, but horror struck again. In order to avoid the taxes, I would have to leave the broken gearbox. Can you imagine that! I decided to wait until Monday so I could see someone of more importance. Happily things worked out and I did

A pretty Intourist guide, Galina Anurina tries out John's TD. Intourist provides all tourists with a guide for part of each day. Quite often the guide is a student looking for practice in languages. Galina was John's guide in Oryol.

get the replacement box as well as being allowed to keep my damaged one. By late afternoon the next day, we were back on the road . . . my TD and I.

During my stay in Bucharest I stayed in an inexpensive hotel. In general, prices were not very high compared to Holland. I was surprised to find many films playing from the West, something I did not find in Russia. From Bucharest I headed north to Brasov where there is a "Black Church", so called because fire damage left its walls black. After Brasov I visited Sighisoara, and old walled town, and the birthplace of Vlad Tepes, the legendary Dracula. After this I went straight to the Yugoslavian border. There it was difficult to believe that I was behind the Iron Curtain. At the border, the customs officer merely asked me if I had anything to declare, stamped my passport and sent me on my way. I had a most pleasant drive along the Adriatic on my way to Italy. In Yugoslavia I experienced no language problems, as many people speak either English or German. One can buy publications from the West as well as Coca-Cola, while there are several marques of automobiles on the road.

I went quickly through Italy and into Switzerland. On my way to Davos I crossed the Fluelapass in a blizzard at 2000 metres. From Davos I went on through the Alps to Grenchen where I had a delightful visit with Rene Rufenacht, the famous M.G. clock repairer, and his wife Susy. From there it was a short trip to Hausach in Germany's Black Forest where I arrived exactly seven weeks and twelve hours after leaving Holland. I arrived in time for the excellent International M.G. Rally held there every three years. From Hausach it was only a short drive home . . . a mere 400 miles.

Here are some technical details of the trip: the TD covered 9375 miles with an average fuel consumption of 10.3 km to the litre (24.5 mpg US or 29.0 mpg UK); I used a total of 8 litres of Duckham's oil, five of which were a complete change. Outside of the gearbox, there were no major problems. I did have a fuel tank leak which I fixed with epoxy, but problems were few. Total cost about $1000; this was possible by camping and by staying out of restaurants.

I have many happy memories of this trip, but I don't intend to retire. Right now I am looking at Africa or perhaps America as possibilities for another interesting journey in my M.G. I know we can do it.

John Bekker

On the previous page (top) is a mountain-top castle which may have been the model for Bram Stoker when he described Count Dracula's habitat. The bottom picture shows additional Rumanian scenery which John Bekker our Dutch adventurer (right) found interesting as well as beautiful

M.A.'S NA

On 21 April 1934, a blue M.G. Magnette (NA Type) two seater tourer was added to the works demonstration fleet, some current models kept by the factory for showing potential customers the magic of M.G. The car was registered JB 3852. Shortly after this, someone was more careless than they should have been, and it disappeared one night; the police, who must have been rather cleverer in those days or perhaps thieves were less clever, eventually traced it, although it had been re-registered DF 8867. This number proved to be forged, and what happened to the thieves is not recorded, but this incident indirectly caused the intended pattern of history for this car to be changed. During its absence from the factory the car had been replaced on the demonstration fleet, and they had a spare car all of a sudden.

Normally at this stage the older car would have been sold, but a journalist called Humfrey Symons had approached Cecil Kimber, M.G.'s Managing Director, for the loan of a car to cover the Alpine Trial. Journalists were a good deal hardier than they are these days (or perhaps manufacturers, then, could trust such souls with valuable cars) for they generally competed in the trials and rallies they reported. Symons was on the staff of *The Motor* and could thus be regarded as able to provide good copy. JB 3852 was duly allotted to him and early in July 1934 an order was given to the M.G. Competition Department to prepare the car for the Alpine Trial.

Modifications included raising the compression ratio to 7.5:1 (standard was 6.2:1), fitting a loud pair of horns and under-car protection for fuel pipes and silencer. The bodywork was given a look over, and the brakes adjusted. This rather casual preparation contrasts with the way in which a car is built up from components for a major rally these days. On 27 July Symons took the car and drove it to and from the rally, collecting a coveted *Coupe des Alpes* for his efforts. Certainly the car behaved well and on its return to the factory was given a comprehensive brake and suspension overhaul; the engine and transmission needed no attention. Now the factory had a non-standard car which was not easily saleable because in 1934 people were not inclined to buy a car which had been thrashed over a rally course. It remained in Abingdon for some time to be used by one or two people for various reasons until, in November, Symons again visited Kimber. This time he wanted to enter the famous Monte Carlo Rally; he had run in every Monte since 1929 and had never done better than finish. In those days the Monte consisted of a run to Monte Carlo from various starting points; penalties were given according to the severity of the expected run—the more difficult the run, the lower the penalty. Penalties were added to by late reporting, but the time schedule by today's standards were fairly easy: an overall average of 35 mph, in lighter traffic conditions than today, but on worse roads. At the end of the run those competitors whose cars were still in fit state could take part in a speed driving test, which in effect really decided the winners from amongst the clean sheets, those whose runs had been penalty-free.

As the accent was on speed in the driving test, Symons maintained that a small car such as the Alpine Magnette with a tuned engine would have the best chance for an outright win, and that the car must be fitted with large-section tyres to help save the suspension and coachwork on the so-called roads of some parts of Europe. It would require a heater and hood. Symons also said that M.G. ought to provide a mechanic to repair the car when necessary as well as covering incidental expenses. An agreement was reached and the car was prepared. Very high power outputs in 1934 were normally attained by supercharging. True, the M.G. which had won the 1934 TT was unblown, and obtained 75 bhp from its 1286 cc engine, but it did use a racing brew for fuel (equivalent to about 85 octane) and had to be kept running fast to eliminate pre-ignition which occurred on this engine due to poor-grade fuel. Kimber, after discussion with Reg Jackson, the Competition Department's Chief Mechanic, decided that a supercharger should be fitted and that the tuning should be for maximum torque at fairly low revs—a primary feature on a blown engine. Eventually a torque of 85 lb/ft was attained at around 3500 rpm; don't forget that this is an engine of under 1300 cc and a maximum of 110 bhp at 6000 rpm was obviously available. The power transmitted through an ENV-built Wilson-type preselector gearbox with a two-plate clutch, although there was no mechanical linkage for the latter, which was expected to slip if too much power was let loose on the unsuspecting gearbox and rear axle.

The rear axle ratio was raised and 5.50 × 16 in. tyres were fitted; this is the first recorded use of the 16 in. wheel on an M.G., a practice which became commonplace on the post-war M.G.s when TC owners found the 19 in. wheels a little too hard riding. The non-standard wheels posed a problem as the spares were too heavy to be carried in the normal place for an NA on the tail, which was only an aluminium sheet. Anyway, they would rather upset

the handling. Eventually they were mounted on either side of the scuttle on special trays. This, in turn, necessitated the fitting of cycle wings, but this proved OK as the French regulations did not allow the standard pattern mud-guard. Snow chains were stowed in the space behind the seats, a speedo fitted in place of the rev counter, and a clock fitted to the dashboard.

All this work was completed in the comparatively short time of two weeks, with the exception of the heater which was never fitted. Good acceleration times were found possible, and a maximum speed of over 100 mph was obtained. The finished car with snow chains and wet weighed over 21 cwt.

Somewhere in the depths of Sweden, almost snowbound and headed for Monte Carlo; the stop was especially for photography—no easy task at sub-zero temperature. On the facing page Harold Parkinson, the first private owner, is pictured competing in a sprint event in 1935.

Even in that form a standing quarter-mile could be done in under twenty seconds. Symons and the M.G. mechanic, Fred Kindell (an irrepressible Cockney who had served with Mercedes before coming to M.G.), sailed for Sweden early in 1935. Sweden in January is not quite so warm as the Costa Brava at the best of times, but in 1935 it was especially cold and Kindell's first job was to lag the sump to prevent the oil from congealing. Once at Umea, the starting city, Symons went to parties while Kindell and the other mechanics had their spirits warmed in the company of their cars, which they were expected to have ready for their masters. One of these apparently dis-

mantled the engine of his Lagonda Rapier during such a garage party, and was so paralytic afterwards that he could not reassemble it . . . and this was the night before the start. Kindell was able to put things right, and by all accounts he was by no means sober. Anyway, suffice to say the driver did not know about this and proceeded.

The M.G. set out for Monte Carlo in the dark of a Swedish morning; imagine driving an open sports car in a rally at forty degrees below freezing. Apart from breaking several snow chains, which were eventually discarded in Stockholm, there were no untoward incidents. Once the 3 cwt of chains were deposited, it was found possible to

average 60 mph on snow all the way to the ferry for Denmark. In Denmark the trip was rather more eventful, for Symons had the misfortune to collide with a Kamikaze cyclist in Copenhagen and wound up in jail, which was probably better than a lynching by the mob, which appeared imminent before the arrival of the police. Fortunately the cyclist was not badly hurt, so Symons was released. After the headlamp glass was replaced (broken by an angry bystander, not the cyclist) off went the intrepid travellers.

Kindell by this time was feeling ill—probably from a lack of sleep coupled with the effects of too much travelling at low temperatures. A stop in Hamburg

On the opposite page is JB 3852 in the non-original condition in which Mike Allison bought it. In the top photo it is seen on its return to Abingdon during the deep freeze of 1962. In the bottom shot the "blue whale" is pictured on its last time out at the 1964 Silverstone race. On this page (top) the fully restored car is captured at Silverstone and at Brands Hatch (bottom) in the wet.

for four hours where they slept in a hotel did something to restore his health, then they were off again. On through Germany, and then into Belgium where they were slowed by fog. Once in France they started to make up time and eventually ran into Monte Carlo having averaged the prescribed 35 mph; in fact, the M.G. was the only car to get to Monte Carlo unpenalised in 1935 so it was in a good position to win the rally outright. All through the night Kindell worked to get the car just right, and then put it in the car park prior to the driving test. Symons elected to drive. At the drop of the flag he leapt in, pressed the starter and found the engine dead; he finally heard Kindell's shouts from the sidelines, leapt out, switched on the battery master switch, and then started the engine. Off he went around the pylons, but as he took the final turn, the car ran into the sandbags. Post-mortem proved that the steering box was broken off from its column, and that this had jammed the steering (some maintain that the accident was caused by excess of *elan*, and the steering broke in consequence of impact, but I keep to the official version). Instead of winning the rally outright, they were placed ninety-eighth, but the M.G. was second in the *Concours de Confort* which followed—a poor recompense.

On its return to the factory (Kindell had fitted a new front axle and steering box and driven the car home) an Eastbourne dealer called Parkinson saw

Memory of a long weekend. We drove to and from the Prescott Hill-Climb in Gloucestershire, one of the most beautiful venues in England, and competed in the climb. During the evening between practice and competition we drove it to a party seventy miles away. How's that for reliability?

JB 3852 and bought her to run in the RAC rally. He won a first-class award. He also competed at Brooklands, but the next phase of activity was a long string of successes in the Brighton Speed Trials. The driver at these pre-war events, Bob Collins, bought it in 1948 and recorded many wins and places in speed events over the next four years until he realized that some of the more modern sports cars had the edge. The solution was a lighter body, which was fitted. Acceleration improved but Davis sold the car in 1952 feeling that it had lost its charm. A whole series of owners then followed, none of whom either improved the car or had any success with it.

In 1959 I first saw it at Richardson's Moor Lane emporium and decided that this was just the thing with which to go vintage car racing. The only snag was that Stan Richardson and I could not agree as to the value. It took nearly two years of negotiation, but finally we agreed to a price in 1961, about the time I was talking to three other enthusiasts about the formation of what became the Triple-M Register. When I got the car home, Wilson McComb told me this was the Monte Carlo car, but at that time the attractions of racing with a reasonably quick M.G. far outweighed any aesthetic considerations.

By 1965, Triple-M had become a big thing, and we were starting to convince

beater, to make up the aluminium panels. He also made the blower cowl which he said was the second he had made for my car; the first was in 1934, so I reckon that is reasonably original. I sprayed the body and then took it to Bill Allen for trimming. The job took the best part of four years to complete.

JB 3852 made her debut in rebuilt form at the M.G. Festival at Silverstone in 1969, but she must have enjoyed her rest since she objected to this new activity and shed a wheel. After a little quiet talking in the garage, I persuaded the car to behave in subsequent events and since then have always started every event entered and only non-finished once, due to a broken valve. Since 1969 the tally is some sixty events, five outright wins, twenty-odd places and a few class wins. The car has also covered something like 25,000 road miles and is an immensely satisfying road car to drive, having almost modern car performance, although something of a dypsomaniac, finding it as difficult to pass petrol stations as her owner does country pubs.

Looking back over the past six years two events have given more satisfaction than all the others: winning the Brook-lands Society Trophy in 1973 and a 33.60 second time at Brighton the following year. The Brighton time represents the best time ever done by the old girl, including when the special body was fitted, as well as being the best time by any standard-bodied Triple-M car for the standing-start kilometre recorded to date. One thing which I still find difficult to believe is how anyone could drive *any* open car 3,000 miles in Northern Europe in January, let alone one without a heater, demisting system, or other aid to comfort, and all in four days of hard motoring.

NA 0307 may not be the prettiest car nor have the aura of a K3, but over the years we have grown attached and learned to forget the few displays of bad manners and remember what enormous fun the car is when in a good mood . . . just like any good mistress. Anne says that as long as she is my only mistress, she doesn't mind; how many other men have such understanding wives?

Mike Allison

owners to keep their cars as original as possible. The secretary could hardly drive a special, so the fateful decision to rebuild it to Monte Carlo trim was taken. Up to this time I had restored it mechanically as near original as possible, fitting a pre-selector gearbox back in place of someone's replacement, but now a body had to be provided. Wilson McComb was able to let me have a copy of the specification sheet raised in 1934, so the job was made much easier than it might otherwise have been. I wrote to all of the previous owners, and Derek Davis was extremely helpful in letting me have all of the original switches and instruments as well as some very useful photographs. The

body, it transpired, had been broken up so there was no alternative but to get another. A second NA was bought, but when I tried to salvage the body it literally fell apart, and all I was able to use were the scuttle top, bonnet, and a few of the cast iron parts. Now I am the sort of person who starts off with a whole forest to make a match; wood and I just do not appear able to form a meaningful working relationship, but my father is very clever in this direction and was able to make a set of pieces necessary to manufacture a body frame. With the help of former M.G. coach-builder Jack Herring, this was soon completed and then I was able to per-suade Billy Wilkins, the M.G. panel-

THE SIGN OF THE OCTAGON

In the following pages you will find some unusual historical material. Ron Cover, a photographer whose work has regularly appeared in this series of annuals, kindly offered to share a publicity booklet which had belonged to his father who had spent a lifetime working for M.G. *M.G. at the Sign of the Octagon* is a rare publication dating from 1932 and was designed to make the factory a place with a personality.

Booklets such as this are rare, as any literature collector will tell you. As can well be imagined, they were not produced in great numbers. Since they were either given away free or sold for a very small sum, the survival rate must be quite slim. This particular booklet reproduced here was one of a series which appeared in the early 1930's. The series told of the racing successes of the M.G. as well as giving testimonies from many satisfied customers.

When *M.G. at the Sign of the Octagon* made its appearance, the factory was probably just settling down to smooth operation after its move from Oxford. Cecil Kimber must have been exceedingly proud of the works and the popular sports cars being produced there. Few men live their dream, but Kimber certainly must have been living his during those early days in Abingdon.

The "Why M.G." item to the right is also of interest because it answers some questions about the origin of the name. Produced before the move to Abingdon, this actually was one page in a sales leaflet for the M Type.

Why MG ?

Out of compliment to SIR WILLIAM MORRIS, Bart., we named our production the M.G. Sports, the letters being the initials of his original business undertaking, "The Morris Garages," from which has sprung that vast group of separate enterprises including

The M.G. Car Company
Oxford

at the Sign
of the Octagon

A Stroll around The M.G. Works

History!

The forerunner of the M.G. Sports. An experimental model turned out in 1923 which gained a Gold Medal in the London—Land's End of that year.

Unique!

" Probably no car has done more to demonstrate that it is possible to combine extremely high road speeds, road holding capabilities and perfect suspension with the ability to crawl through traffic at five miles an hour and behave in every way like the town carriage, than the M.G. Sports. This is a car which has set something approaching a new standard in motoring, which has won the admiration of engineers, pioneer motorists and newcomers alike."

Mr. J. H. Perry, the well known
Motoring Correspondent.

The first production model M.G. Sports, 1924.

Introduction

So many people still do not realise, the transition being so rapid, that The M.G. Car Company is now one of the largest leading Manufacturers of Sports Cars, and that their productions are to exclusive M.G. design, and not to be confused with the productions of any other of the companies controlled by Sir William R. Morris, Bart.

It is to help people to appreciate this fact that the following pages were written and illustrated.

Personnel

M.G. Sports Cars have advanced from success to success during the last few years, gradually taking a higher place among the Sporting Cars of the world.

The reason for this is the enthusiasm that permeates the Factory, from the Managing Director to the newest apprentice and which is built into every car we produce.

Visitors, on entering the factory, meet first one and then another of the staff and find the friendly atmosphere of enthusiasm most contagious.

On walking around the Works, in all departments may be seen men putting into their work that little bit extra that counts for so much.

Even the Service Manager has a smile for his visitors, and, as a matter of fact, the M.G. service goes a long way towards making the owners so enthusiastic.

Such a band of keen specialists can only produce a sports car of the very highest calibre and this is borne out by the wonderful racing successes recently achieved and the large number of satisfied owners.

Sir William R. Morris, Bt., and our Managing Director, Mr. Cecil Kimber, on the former's first tour of inspection of the new Works at Abingdon.

The phenominal rise to fame of the M.G. Sports Cars.

In 1924 a limited number of M.G. Sports Cars were produced in a small mews in Oxford.

The owners of these early productions—which were quite frankly 'hotted-up' editions of the well known Morris Oxford chassis, but fitted with special coachwork—were so enthusiastic in their praise that the demand quickly necessitated a move to larger premises in 1926.

The mews in Pusey Lane where the first M.G.'s were produced.

This new factory was situated in Bainton Road, North Oxford. Here cars were produced in considerably larger numbers, only to be eagerly purchased by an increasing coterie of M.G. enthusiasts, and the infection

The Bainton Road Factory.

grew to such an extent that by the autumn of 1927 it was found necessary

to build a £20,000 factory; this being situated at Edmund Road, Cowley, not far from the main works of Morris Motors Ltd.

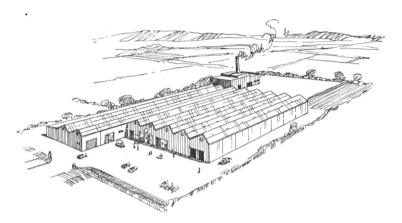

The Edmund Road Works.

By this time such considerable modifications were introduced to the chassis and engine of the Morris Oxford that the car gradually took on, what might be termed, more than ever of an M.G. personality.

Again the demand increased and again the factory accommodation was found insufficient to cope with it and still another move was undertaken. This to an ideally situated and already existing factory at Abingdon-on-Thames, and here, with the introduction of the M.G. Six and the M.G. Midget, we became a Motor Manufacturing Concern with a separate entity, building these cars, using engines and chassis of exclusive M.G. design, by a new kind of flow production method, in which each car is built with individual care, as if it was the only one being manufactured.

This care, plus the exclusive M.G. design, is responsible for the marvellous M.G. performances which have impressed everyone so much. At these Works we are always ready to welcome visitors and to show them round what is possibly the largest and finest factory in the World exclusively devoted to the production of Sporting Motor Cars.

We will now introduce you to our Managing Director, Mr. Cecil Kimber, who will, in imagination, personally conduct you on a tour of inspection around the works.

PETER CROSBY

Aerial view of the Works at Abingdon.

Just in case you are unable to come to these Works of which we are so proud, or, having come, have not had the opportunity of being shown round properly, I want you to accompany me in imagination on a tour.

The Service reception department

Leaving the modest and unassuming office block behind you—only notable perhaps for having the Managing Director's Office furnished and decorated in a somewhat novel style in which a Tudor fireplace and oak beams are the outstanding features—we walk down to the Service Reception Department, possibly the most important in the Works, isolated from the busy, sometimes hectic; rush of the Main Works, where everyone receives quiet, individual and undivided attention. Here you can bring your car and be interviewed in warmth and comfort by a staff, who themselves own M.G. Cars, and whose only desire is to be really helpful, whether your car is not running quite to your satisfaction or whether you have been unfortunate enough to " bend " your " Barouche." Filed in this Department is the life history of every car we have ever built with a record of all its owners, all its troubles and all its trials. This priceless information is analysed, tabulated and used by our Design and Development Department to make M.G. Cars better and better.

The Boiler House

Before coming to the Works proper let us enter what surely must be the cleanest boiler house in existence, using coal. Over £5,000 was spent on this steam heating plant, but it provides ideal working conditions during the coldest and dampest weather, all helping towards the high quality of our M.G. production.

The Car Wash.

Coming out of the boiler house and tucked away in an odd corner is our little laundry. This deals with the washing and drying of some hundreds of overalls and dozens of car sheets, towels, etc., per week, making it possible for everyone to start the week cleanly clad and live up to our high standard of cleanliness which contributes so largely to efficiency. Leaving the laundry and noting the high pressure washing plant we walk along the well lit and warmed wash, where all cars, whether new ones or old ones in for service—are cleaned on receipt and again cleaned and polished before being handed over to their owners.

The Works proper

Then at last we come to the Works proper. To obtain a comprehensive view the best plan is to walk up the new ramp constructed for taking cars to the body section. Half way up here a fine inclusive view of almost the whole works is obtained. In the immediate foreground are the three assembly lines.

The Ramp.

In principle they follow the logical floor production method, but here you will find no geared conveyor setting a speed to the work. Instead each job has to be done well and done properly however long it may take. On the right are the finished part Production Stores in the best position for feeding out to the line, and on the left the Stores, similarly placed, for feeding the line with the heavy units—frames, engines and axles. From the upper floor to the commencement of the assembly line will be seen a chute for wheels and tyres.

In the distance will be seen the Rectification, Road Test, Final Test and Final Finishing Sections.

The Body Shop

Proceeding further " up the hill " we reach a floor devoted to the storage of tyres, wheels and bodies. The short sub-assembly lines will be noticed. These take charge of the wiring and finishing off of both the M.G. Open and Closed bodies, before these are dropped down on a slung platform to be mounted on the waiting chassis passing along the line below. The further end of the upper floor is a coachwork repair section where on a tiled floor and with a well lighted roof the acme of ideal working conditions is reached.

We will now descend to the ground level noting the rows of finished engines waiting to be assembled into chassis. A thought given to the probable cost of each engine and a small sum in mental arithmetic makes one realise how very much capital is involved in the modern manufacture of motor cars.

Assembly Department.

The Assembly Lines

We find ourselves now on the assembly line. Let us turn to the right and get down to the start where a chassis in an upside down position is being fitted with axles and springs. A sling device then turns it right side up ready for the engine to be dropped in. A walk up the line reveals the meticulous care that makes each operation appear quite

leisurely. This gives one an opportunity of studying the sturdiness of the design, the fine cross-bracing of the chassis, the clever lubrication of all moving parts and, for those who can see it, the underlying reason why the M.G. possesses such stability at speed.

The Test Department

At the end of the assembly line we now turn to the right and find the road test and rectification section. The former is provided with three

Testing Department.

interesting devices well worth examination. One is a wheel alignment indicator. A shallow platform has on its surface two longitudinal plates with sideway movement. A tester runs a car across this and if the front wheels are out of alignment these plates are forced sideways recording the amount of the misalignment on a large dial carried on a pedestal. The speed and accuracy of this device entirely eliminates the liability of error due to the human element when the old fashioned trammels are used.

Adjoining this you will see the Bendix Cowdrey brake testing machine, another device which eliminates the old fashioned "hit or miss" method of adjusting brakes. As you will see the car is run on to the rollers and anchored by its front axle. Each little set of rollers is rotated by a separate electric motor. Upon the brakes being applied the torque resistance of each wheel is shown individually on four dials. Separate brake adjustment then provides the necessary equalisation of effort, and at this stage, the setting of headlamps—to avoid the sky or hedge-row searching beams—is perfected by careful registering on a calibrated screen. All cars and chassis after undergoing a long road test, during

The Rectification Department.

which process they may go back to the rectification section a number of times, are then proved out on our special high speed test rig or Comparator. The rear wheels of the car or chassis are run on to the large diameter rollers sunk into the floor. Upon the car being driven these rollers are rotated and in their turn drive a large air fan enclosed in a case. The resistance of this fan has been carefully worked out and the resultant speeds, on all gears, are comparable (hence Comparator) with the road speeds shown on the special speedometer. No matter how long the preliminary running in and testing may take, each car has to pass a definite standard speed. Further careful running in by the owner should give a still improved performance.

The Finishing Section

Having passed " Rectification," we can note the final finishing Department to which the cars are passed before going to the Despatch. The Finishing Section is arranged conveniently close to our Cellulosing Department, which we will walk through next. A fine lofty shop, white tiled with the very latest equipment for spray and cellulosing. Coming out of this shop which smells so strongly of the pear drops of our childhood days, we can pay a brief visit to a number of compact shops opening out of the main floor.

An M.G. Midget in the London to Barnstable Trial 1930.

The Maintenance Department

Here you will see a snug little carpenter's shop. Overhead lives the Plant Maintenance Engineer directing his Millwrights, Electricians, Bricklayers, Plumbers, Carpenters, Steam Engineers, without whose quiet and unobtrusive presence the Works could not continue, and almost next door is the Mess Room, providing comfortable accommodation and equipment toward maintaining the human efficiency without which Works efficiency would be impossible.

The Tool Store

Then let us ask the Tool store-keeper to let us walk round his neatly arranged racks with their bewildering variety of contents, and see also our First Aid Section, providing that necessary immediate help by a fully competent St. John's Ambulance Member, in all cases however small, where promptitude often saves serious after effects.

The Machine Shop and Welding Department

We will now visit the machine shop, first of all we notice the absence of the mass of overhead belting which is usually found in this type of shop. Here all pulleys are carried on underground shafting and short belts drive the various machines.
First of all we will watch chassis side members being accurately and quickly drilled with the help of jigs which render mistakes impossible.

In this department also we can see speedometers and oil gauges being tested for accuracy on an ingenious machine—brake linings also receive attention and are bedded in thoroughly before the axles leave for the assembling department, and here the numerous components which are built into the cars all undergo exacting tests to ensure that only the very finest of materials are used.

The Machine Shop and Chassis Frame Making Department.

A glance will suffice for the hundred and one jobs of machining which are carried out, but before we pass on to the next department we must ask the foreman to show us into the blacksmith's shop to look at the automatic oxy-acetylene plant which quickly cuts sheet steel of various thicknesses to the required shape.

Frame Making Department

The Frame making department now calls for our attention, this shop has a Jacobean setting of roughly hewn oak beams and pillars; as we enter we are almost deafened by noise from the busy pneumatic rivetting machines.

The Chassis Frame Assembly Department.

To this department the chassis side members are passed, having already been dealt with by the machine shop, and together with the tubular cross bracings are set up on a special fixture and held in place by location clamps—two rivets are then placed in position on opposite sides of the frame, and a novel type of pneumatic expanding dolly placed against the two heads—air is introduced to this dolly which firmly holds the rivets home. A pneumatic hammer at each side completes the operation. On every chassis twelve pairs of rivets are dealt with in this manner. A few rivets cannot be dealt with in this way and have to be treated individually, in which case the rivet heads register with stationary dollys mounted on the chassis table.

The completed frames are finally numbered and passed to the production department.

The Power Unit Shop

As we enter this department, the pride of a scrupulously tidy foreman, we note the row of test beds, beautifully clean and paved with white tiles, also the octagonal facia boards, and the watchful mechanic alert for the very tiniest 'spot of bother' on the units which are happily humming away doing the equivalent of some of those unpleasant running-in miles.

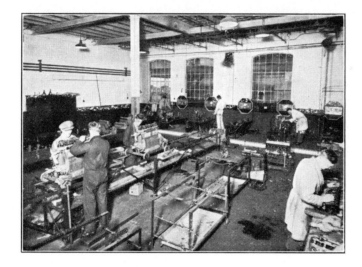

The Power Unit Shop.

We will now look at the units on their assembly line, here we see besides the various constructional operations, the testing under pressure of water jackets, oil pipes, gearboxes being fitted, clutches adjusted, and finally, the manifolds are given a coat of heat resisting paint, and the whole unit is cellulosed—we believe in appearance as well as performance. The units are now ready for the assembling department.

Unit repairs are also catered for here and the 'motors' with many miles to their credit rejuvenated.

The Experimental Department

This department, known as the " Hush Hush " Section, is not normally open to visitors, but in imagination let us walk through and see numbers of cars under construction that certainly are not like the Production models we have seen on the Assembly line.   These are built up under the eagle eyes of the Experimental Foreman and the Chief Draughtsman, who presides over the drawing office which overlooks this shop   This fusing of the practical and theoretical is not usual, but the friendly rivalry that exists between the two sections produces really good results.   Much good drawing paper is saved by this method.

Leaving the drawing office with sheets discreetly shielding some of its drawing boards and having noted the strategic position of the General Manager's Office, we will now walk down the main gangway as far as the Service Repair Shop.

The Service Repair Shop

Here come the lame ducks with the battered radiators and front axles askew. Also those cars suffering from nothing more serious than a touch of indigestion. Along the right of this bay will be noticed the Service Stores.

The Service Repair Shop.

Over £10,000 worth of parts is in this compact little store, but this and the Service Repairs bay are entirely separate from the Production side of the Works so that one never interferes with the other. Leaving the patients to the ministrations of their doctor, the Service Superintendent.

The Despatch Department

We will now go on to the Despatch Department, and have our eyes gladdened by rows of nice new shiny motor cars all ready waiting for their lucky future owners. It is hard to say which is the more attractive, the stately row of M.G. Sixes or the colourful ranks of the Magnas and Midgets.

Despatch Department.

Electrical Section

Before leaving this domain we must just put our heads into a little shop where an electrician not only watches over the sub-station but sees that every battery on every new car that leaves the Works is really fully charged. A small point but quite important to the future content of the new owner, and on our way back to the Main Entrance, we cannot refrain from pointing out to you the expanse of land available at the rear of the Works for future developments. Here garage accommodation is provided for the large number of employees' motor cars, motor cycles and homely push-bikes. See also our Aerial sign and Wind Direction flag giving guidance to flying owner-friends who frequently visit us by air, landing in the adjacent aerodrome.

And so our trip comes to an end but before leaving Abingdon if you have time, go and see some of the fine old buildings that the town possesses. The Guildhall is well worth a visit.

A batch of Midgets leaving the Works.

Goodbye. Hope we see you again soon when you come for your next new car.

THE WORKS
TODAY

It would be entirely possible to take *M.G. at the Sign of the Octagon* and use it fairly successfully as a guide to the works today. Things, of course, are not the way they used to be, but much of the old remains and contributes to the present charm. A great deal of expansion has taken place at the works since the close of World War II. When the export potential of the marque was discovered with the success of the TC and TD, it became apparent that added production facilities were necessary. It is somehow fitting that some of the additions to floor space were actually constructed utilizing American packing case lumber which had arrived during the war in large quantities.

Newer buildings to the west of the original factory now house the following departments: Rectification, Dispatch, Special Tuning, Development and Design. These brick structures occupy what was once a sort of test track.

The "friendly atmosphere of enthusiasm" which was noted in *M.G. at the Sign of the Octagon* is still evident at the factory. The most outstanding evidence of this spirit is in the work record of the employees. The nationalized British Leyland Ltd, of which M.G. is a part, is well known for an almost continuous succession of labour disputes. Lost time from strikes is accepted as being perfectly normal at every branch except Abingdon. The M.G. workers have the best record of any British Leyland firm and it may well be the best production

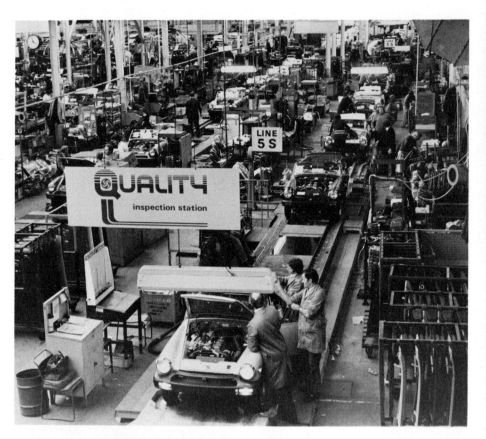

The Midget line (top) closest to the camera. At this end of the line the cars are complete and ready for roller-testing and inspection. The MGB line (bottom) is located in what used to be the Service Department. On the facing page (top) we see the fully trimmed and painted body shells at the start of their assembly process. In the bottom photo the cars are a little further along.

crew in all of British industry. Why this is true can be explained, in part, by the existence of an intangible something which was implanted by Cecil Kimber and nurtured over the years by men such as Cecil Cousins, John Thornley, Syd Enever, Reg Jackson and their contemporaries. M.G. is a small establishment as automobile factories go, and it is located in a small city. As such the work force is static and many second, and even third, generation workers are employed there. This father-to-son tradition is a contributing factor to the spirit at Abingdon. Added to this is a feeling of independence from the other British Leyland units, which is extremely important in maintaining their admirable willingness to produce a quality sports car. In Abingdon men talk about working at the G's; the pride with which they say it is very obvious.

The present managing director is Robert Ward. He came to Abingdon in the autumn of 1974 after a varied career in the automobile industry. Bob Ward did not come up through the ranks at Abingdon and may have been unaware of the spirit which exists there. He quickly became attuned to the existing enthusiasm and is proud of the continued atmosphere of pride of workmanship which the more than 1000 men of M.G. display.

Visits to the works are no longer a matter of merely dropping in as they were in the 1930's. Tours are rarely given to individuals, but it is sometimes possible to arrange a group tour. Every M.G. enthusiast should make an effort to visit the works at least once.

One should keep in mind that the M.G. factory is really an assembly plant. Various components come in from all areas of England and are assembled at Abingdon. The bodies, for example, are stamped out at Swindon and sent to Cowley for trimming (soon trimming will be done in Abingdon). They are then sent to Abingdon for completion. The engines come from Longbridge and the drive train is from Birmingham. Others bits, as mentioned, are produced in factories all over England.

Painted and trimmed bodies enter the works on the second floor of the assembly building and are placed on dollies. It is interesting to note that these dollies are all advanced by hand; there is no automatic, continuously moving conveyor belt, and this adds to the hand-assembled reputation. Instruments, wiring looms and brake pipes are all installed on the second floor before the shells are lifted down to the ground floor. On this level the engine and drive train are fitted, and the car is completed. Before leaving the assembly building each car is roller-tested. In the old days every car was road-tested, but the sheer volume today precludes that. Random cars are tried on the road, and all are thoroughly checked on the roller machine.

A very close inspection reveals which cars need to go to the Rectification Department in order to be put right before shipment. All faults are carefully dealt with before the cars are released. A small scratch in the paint, for example, will usually mean that an entire panel is refinished.

There is no longer a Service Department at Abingdon. It was housed in the area which is now an MGB assembly line in the bay closest to Marcham Road. That line was at one time the MGC line.

About 1200 MGBs and Midgets are produced each week; that is a bit better than one car for each employee. More cars are being completed than ever before. Early in 1976 a significant milestone was reached when the one-millionth car to be built at Abingdon rolled off the line. It probably will not be long before the millionth M.G. will be completed, and the MGB must certainly be reaching the half-million mark. With production figures such as these, the claim that M.G. is the world's most popular sports car is justified. It has always been America's best-selling sports car. Early in 1977 an over-zealous British Leyland public relations department put out a news release that Triumph had outsold M.G. in the USA in 1976. That was a difficult pill to swallow when one considers that Leyland put a ceiling on M.G. production and most American dealers had hundreds of unfilled orders. Yet, facts are facts—or are they? What actually happened was that the release which claimed

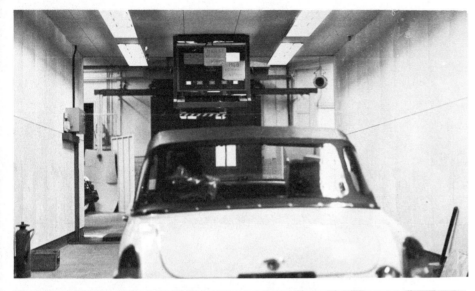

Triumph sales superiority was based on British Leyland's optimistic shipment of several thousand more Triumphs than M.G.s to the States. The release should have said that for the first time in history more Triumphs than M.G.s were sent to America. And so there is a story to be finished. All of the M.G.s were sold. The Triumphs? I thought you'd never ask. At this writing there are several *thousand* unsold Triumphs on their way from America to Europe in the hopes that they can be sold there. And M.G. is still the undisputed leader in sports car sales in USA.

An M.G. Competitions Department no longer exists; there is, however, a Leyland Special Tuning Department based there. This group maintains current factory competition efforts as well as doing work for customers as required. The pre-war Competitions Department was located on the second floor of the main assembly building where present cars have instruments and electrics fitted. The present tuning shop is a far cry from the glorious days of the pre-1935 all-out M.G. racing efforts. Even today, however, there is some of that heritage present and one feels a bit of history when visiting this department.

The Design Staff and entire drawing office crew returned to Abingdon from Cowley in 1954. They had been moved there in 1935 and were happy to return to make the MGA and MGB true Abingdon designs. Housed with them is the Engineering Office. A major function of this group is meeting changing world governmental regulations. They also do the crash and roll-over testing right at Abingdon. Further, they do the design refinements to existing models necessitated each year. One wonders if this division is working on an MGB replacement.

The works today is an exciting place where one can still view a good sports car being hand-assembled. While there is a minimum of wasted time or effort, one does not come away with the feeling that the M.G. is a mass-produced item. Above all is that feeling of history and that Octagon Spirit which exists in Abingdon.

Dick Knudson

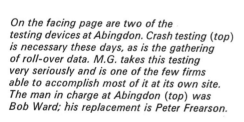

On the facing page are two of the testing devices at Abingdon. Crash testing (top) is necessary these days, as is the gathering of roll-over data. M.G. takes this testing very seriously and is one of the few firms able to accomplish most of it at its own site. The man in charge at Abingdon (top) was Bob Ward; his replacement is Peter Frearson.

ADO 23:
THE B
GOES ON

The world's most successful sports car is the MGB. Strong words? Yes. Unsubstantiated? No. Consider the facts—no other sports car has been produced in such numbers nor remained in production for so many years. The MGB has introduced more people to sports car motoring than any other marque in production.

As soon as most of the engineering problems of the MGA were solved in late 1955, Syd Enever and his staff started thinking of the future. Syd had been with M.G. since the pre-1930 days in Oxford; a practical engineer with an innate creative genius, he learned his craft on the shop floor and became the firms' Chief Engineer.

Syd Enever was largely responsible for the design of EX135, the K3-based car with which Goldie Gardner captured many speed records before and after World War II. Highly aware of the advantages of an aerodynamic shape, Syd inspired the firm to make its first production break with the square-rigged concept when the MGA went into production in 1955. The MGA

shape was an Enever invention which first appeared on a TD chassis as a one-off special for George Phillips to drive in the 1951 Le Mans race. This improved shape added over 30 mph to the top speed and foreshadowed future designs.

Two other record-breakers with efficient aerodynamic shapes appeared in the mid-1950's and earned their place in the history of speed. EX179 and EX181 used TF and MGA engines to break several records: indeed, Phil Hill became the fastest man ever in an M.G. with a speed of 254.91 mph in the twin-cam EX181 in September 1959. Coupling the success of the record-breakers with the world-wide enthusiastic acceptance of the MGA it is not too difficult to understand the development of the MGB design. To say that one particular predecessor motivated the MGB would be an over simplification; the MGB evolved from years of successful Enever thinking. The roundness of the body design was Syd's basic means of adhering to the principles of aerodynamics and its

maturation as a viable body shape can be traced over the years since the pre-war record-breakers. The concept may have reached its ultimate in EX181, but it certainly existed prior to this time in other cars.

According to Peter Neal of the works design staff, the basic design philosophy was to produce what Syd wanted. Peter, an apprentice draughtsman at the time, actually did the first styling art of the MGB based largely on some "fag packet" rough sketches done by Syd in moments of inspiration. After this a couple of wooden models were constructed followed by more of what Syd called "pretty pictures". Syd then took this artwork and a one-quarter scale outline to the BMC headquarters at Longbridge. On the strength of these drawings, BMC commissioned Frua to build a prototype on an MGA chassis. When the Frua car was returned to Abingdon, it was deemed to be too much Frua; as such, it was turned down. Once again Syd started to feed his staff ideas. Abingdon's master modelmaker, Harry Herring, artfully translated the drawings

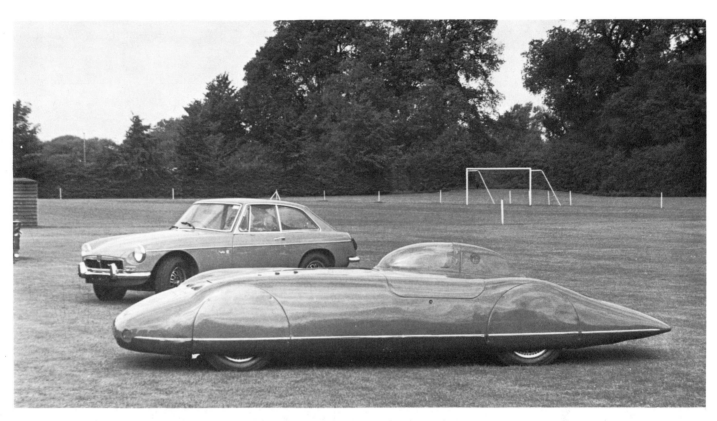

On the facing page are two Enever creations which obviously influenced the MGB. EX179 (top) is shown with a V8 GT in the background. UMG 400 was the TD-based forerunner of the MGA which was built for Le Mans. Alec Hounslow is behind the wheel. Henry Stone is second from the left beside Syd Enever. The Frua design (above) was meant to be a replacement for the MGA but was not accepted at Abingdon.

of John O'Neill, Chief Body Designer, and Don Hayter, Chief Draughtsman. Syd was always on top of this design work and was able to see his original concept grow into the successful MGB. At this point, Peter Neal did some more styling art which Syd took to the BMC chief, Leonard Lord. Not only did Lord like what he saw, but he also decided to keep the art to decorate his office walls. In the late summer of 1959, detailed one-quarter scale drawings were completed, and it only remained to build a prototype. It is interesting to note that the marketing division did not influence the design at all.

There seems little doubt that this was an Abingdon design. That being the

case, the MGB will probably be the last M.G. to be conceived there. The people most involved in the actual design would include the fifty or so employees of the design and development divisions. The Managing Director of M.G. at that time was John Thornley, to whom Syd Enever was directly responsible; Syd's reputation by that time was so golden that he virtually had a free hand. Other key personnel included, Jim O'Neill, Chief Body Designer; Don Hayter, Chief Body Draughtsman; Roy Brocklehurst, Chief Chassis Draughtsman; and Terry Mitchell, Chief Chassis Designer.

Knowing full well the popularity of the MGA coupe, it was only natural to follow it with a GT version of the MGB.

Interestingly enough, the GT was completely designed shortly after the roadster; it was not just some after-thought appearing three years after the open version was introduced in 1962. Once again the Longbridge directors decided to let a foreign designer, this time Farina, have a go at the styling. To complete the GT design, Abingdon sent the roadster drawings, together with their suggested outline for the coupe, to Farina, who gave it what has become a timeless GT treatment. On close inspection, there are two distinct schools of design present in the GT which harmonize artistically rather than clash with each other. The crisp, straight lines of Farina are in curious contrast

with Enever's roundness, but the blend of the two has produced a classic shape still much in demand today.

After the Longbridge go-ahead on the AD023 project, it took almost three years for the prototype to be built. It was tested extensively at the nearby Chalgrove Aerodrome, where it was revealed that the major difficulty to overcome was scuttle shake, a common fault in open two-seaters. This was solved by fitting a reinforcing tube behind the facia. Other problems were virtually non-existent because, according to the Abingdon design staff, "the MGB was well-engineered because Syd was so thorough".

A sharp drop in sales of the MGA in

Another experimental shape is shown in the above photograph. Happily the decision was made to go with the Abingdon-designed MGB (opposite and following pages). The correctness of that decision is emphasized by the sales record of the MGB since its introduction in the autumn of 1962. No other sports car to date has matched its popularity.

1961 brought about the introduction of the MGB in 1962. The design office considered such things as an egg-crate grille and two-tone colour schemes; in the end, however, they realized that the sports car customer of the 1960's wanted wind-up windows and a few more of the creature comforts that only a re-design could provide.

Welcomed by the press and public alike, the MGB went on to become the world's most popular sports car. Production figures follow this article, but by the end of its production run we are apt to see a half-million MGBs.

The major obstacle which almost caused the demise of the MGB was the introduction of America's infamous federal regulations, which appeared in 1969. For a time it was uncertain if the works could meet the US requirements; that they did is a credit to the design staff at Abingdon. At first the regulations appeared overwhelming; the simple fact was that if the regulations could not be met at a reasonable cost, then the US market would have been dropped. For a three-month period no US cars were made while an all-out effort was made to make the changes America was requiring of all manufacturers. Many men were laid off, with only the non-American assembly lines continuing to work in this grim time. In the end every requirement was met; in fact, M.G. was the only foreign car to meet all of the regulations sincerely. In many instances they exceeded the demands.

There were minor changes over the years. The designers do not point to any particular year as being better but consider them all good. Enthusiasts, on the other hand, point to the cars with leather interiors and the five-main-bearing engine as being the most desirable of models.

The motoring press has motivated few changes over the years. We could point to the addition of an ashtray as standard equipment, the fitting of face-level vents, and the substitution of a smaller steering wheel as evidence of an open ear at Abingdon.

Grille and trim changes occurred at various times to deal with changes in fashion and to cater to the whims of the buying public; some worked and some

The MGB/GT was not released until 1965 even
though it was designed much earlier. It is
a tasteful blend of Enever roundness and
Farina straightness which has produced a
classic shape. The hardtop roadster on the
facing page is shown ready for Le Mans (top)
and at a hill-climb (bottom) after having
had a face-lift. The MGB has proved
itself in club racing many times.

In good company, the ex-Donald Healey
MGB (top) is flanked by a smart MGA
on one side and the purposeful looking
ex-Maurice Toulmin PB Cream Cracker. Racing
MGBs (bottom) today are often much modified.

did not—the black grille being a case in
point. But these were not major changes.
The largest outcry came when the so-
called "rubber bumpers" were fitted in
1975. These massive devices were a
compromise with the American regulations and caused a change in basic
appearance which almost everyone
accepts as commonplace today.

One of the most interesting versions of
the MGB was the V8-engined car
introduced in 1973. Using the aluminium
Rover engine, the MGB/GT was trans-
formed into an extremely sophisticated
grand touring car. A popular V8 conversion was being done by Ken Costello
in Kent as early as 1971. Receiving rave
reviews by a variety of road-testers of

This grille change was not the most successful modification of the basic design. It was irreverently called the "black hole" at the works and did not last long. There really have been few major changes in what was a basically sound design from the very beginning.

the various automobile magazines, it was little wonder that this conversion attracted Leyland's attention. When Costello went to Sir Donald Stokes with a request for more engines, Stokes decided that it was about time Abingdon joined the V8 picture. He instructed the design office to start production as soon as possible, and it was designed in double-quick time. Engine modifications included new inlet manifolding plus a different oil pump. Making that eight-cylinder engine fit into a space originally designed for a four took some shoehorning, but the end result was a masterpiece of space utilization. All subsequent Bs eventually had the same engine compartment as the V8's.

Cost estimates on tooling for the V8 option run as high as £250,000; admittedly, accurately determining exact costs on such a project is impossible, but we know it was expensive. Originally production projections were for 100 cars a week with fifty of them going to America. The works certainly had the technical ability to meet US specifications, and there was a ready market in

the States for this marvellous motor car. In the end the USA version was never manufactured and the UK model was subsequently cut. The official position of Leyland was that there did not exist sufficient manpower to produce the engines needed for the Rover and the M.G., so the M.G. V8 was axed. While this official reasoning may seem logical on first hearing, it just does not hold up under close scrutiny. Consider the following:

1. 1975—the MGB/GT no longer exported to America.
2. 1975—the Triumph TR-7 is introduced to America.
3. 1976—the MGB/GT no longer exported to Europe.
4. 1976—the TR-7 is introduced to Europe.
5. 1976—the MGB V8 is cancelled.
6. 1977—the TR-7 V8 version is introduced?

Company politics are really only understood fully by high executives within that company; from an enthusiast's point of view, however, it would

The MGB/GT V8 is certainly one of the best cars ever to come out of Abingdon. It was motivated by very successful conversions done by Costello Motor Engineering in Kent (opposite, top). Now that production of the V8 has ceased at Abingdon, Costello is back in business.

seem that Leyland may have erred in the establishment of their priorities concerning the MGB and the TR-7. The proven world-wide demand for the MGB contrasts vividly with the lack of public response to the TR-7; the philosophy of "the public be damned" seems more in keeping with the tycoons of Detroit than with the gentlemen of Leyland in Longbridge.

Considering the obvious emphasis on the Triumph, one wonders when the end will come for MGB. The 16 December 1976 edition of the *Abingdon Herald* carried a front-page article which quoted a Leyland spokesman as saying that in view of increased American sales they would continue to produce it as long as sales held up. The British motoring press has been forecasting the finish of the marque for some time. One highly regarded journal published a brief article in 1976 which claimed the works would close in 1977 because the long-term lease of the buildings and land would expire then. This journal claimed that Leyland would not continue in premises they did not own and that the marque

Two significant milestones at Abingdon are shown here. In the top photo we see the 250,000th MGB roll off the line on 27 May 1971. It was driven off by George Turnbull, then Managing Director of British Leyland's Austin Morris Division. The bottom photo shows Captain George Eyston beside the 1,000,000th car built at Abingdon— not all of them, of course, have been M.G.s. On the facing page (top) is one of the limited-edition Golden Anniversary GTs. The addition of a hardtop (bottom) makes a roadster quite snug in the winter.

Facing are two men who were instrumental in producing the MGB. John Thornley (left) was Managing Director of M.G. while Syd Enever (right) was in charge of its design. Seated in the EX181 record-breaker is the famous Stirling Moss. That Abingdon looked to the future is evident in the above shot of EX234 which was a possible MGB replacement. It is now in the Syd Beer Collection.

was as good as dead. This report was untrue. The buildings and land are owned by the works; in fact, there is even an option on adjoining land should there be a need to expand. Interestingly enough, Leyland never disputed that article. One can only assume that they let it stand in order to serve as a readily acceptable excuse should they decide to call it quits.

But will they? What does the future hold? It is conceivable that Leyland may decide to put the famous Octagon on a version of the TR-7. The result of that sort of marketing ploy is difficult to predict, but it appears that the strength of the Octagon Spirit is about to be tested.

On this page are side and rear views of a full-size wooden model of one of the earliest Syd Enever concepts of the MGB. This Abingdon design developed from the earliest styling drawings (see photo page 82). On the facing page (top) is a styling drawing (probably done by Dick Burzi at Longbridge) of a Farina Magnette with a Frua grille; it didn't help much, but management was trying to salvage something from the aborted Frua effort. The quarter-scale model (bottom) is a part of the MGB's evolution.

PRODUCTION DATA

Year	Number produced	Changes
1962	4,518	Introduced
1963	23,308	Optional overdrive, stronger brake lever, modified rear springs optional hardtop
1964	26,542	Oil cooler, five main bearings, electric tach, crankcase breather
1965	24,179	Sealed prop shaft, 12-gallon fuel tank, GT introduced
1966	22,675	Front anti-roll bar standard
1967	15,457	Fully synchronized gearbox for Mk II, back-up lights, door trim and seats revised, automatic transmission optional
1968	25,704	
1969	31,030	Black grille, leather-rimmed steering wheel, reclining front seats optional
1970	36,570	Interior courtesy light, steering lock, improved ventilation, self-locking boot and bonnet, stays
1971	34,680	Mk III introduced, centre console rocker switches, armrest, collapsible steering column (US) nylon seat inserts on GT
1972	39,396	New grille with original chrome rim, nylon seats on GT, seatbelt warning system
1973	30,823	New badges
1974	30,205	Rubber bumpers, raised suspension, 12 V battery
1975	N/A	
1976	N/A	(mid-1976) Zip-in rear window, deck-chair seats and halogen headlamps on UK cars, new facia panel

A MAN
CALLED
MILLER

The name Miller is synonomous in South Africa with not only motor racing, but also M.G., for no other person has done as much to promote the Octagon and Maintain the Breed in the truest sense of the word in this country as Les Miller. He devoted almost his entire racing career to carrying aloft the M.G. banner, and his post-war stable was to identify totally with M.G. as the words "Ecurie Miller—M.G." after each car entered was to proclaim in racing programmes across the country.

Les cut his racing teeth in a little BSA three-wheeler in which he entered numerous hill-climb events in the Durban area and grass-track races at Curries Fountain. This exclusive to Natal shoe-string type motor racing provided many thrills for motor sport fans in the early thirties and motor-cycle-and-sidecars were matched with doorless light cars to provide passenger machine contests. In 1934, his first year of competitive driving, Les proved without doubt that he would be the one to watch, being the only record-breaker at the Natal Motor Cycle Club event at New Germany on 16 September though coming second to Norcott on a Levis 500 sidecar with a run of 23 seconds dead. This feat was regarded by the motoring press as fantastic, as it was only his second appearance on the "hill". On 6 October, he competed in the Killerby Cup Knock-Out Hill-Climb and, although denied the laurels once more, again broke the record.

In 1935, Miller won the NMCC event at New Germany on 23 February, and broke his existing record handsomely with a run of 21.3 seconds. Coming second on 23 March to Basil Cook's Austin 7 in a grass-track event at Curries Fountain, he won the second heat of the mixed race in incredible style, losing the final to King's "wonderful little M.G." as the *Week-End Advertiser* described it. Earlier in the meeting Cook's Austin 7 and King's J2 Midget had touched at speed; Cook's Austin left the track, and King's "wonderful little M.G., thanks to perfect road-holding and weight distribution, swung clean around and never looked like overturning"—the press had already recognized a thoroughbred. All Miller

needed now, of course was an M.G.

In Les Miller's scrapbook, above a picture of Lionel Meyer posing with his M.G. Magnette and mechanics after coming fourth in the second South African Grand Prix, is the simple inscription: "This started it all". Above a picture of King's M.G. is the statement "My first drive in an M.G."

In 1936 Les Miller appeared with his first M.G.—an L Type Magna—and on 8 March behind the wheel of this car he won the Indian Shield with a run of 46.3 seconds—nearly two seconds faster than the runner-up. This was also the year of ARDS—The Arrow Drivers Stable. Les Miller, inspired with the idea of starting a South African racing

A smiling Les Miller (above) receives the coveted Barnes Trophy for his great drive in the 1952 East London Winter Handicap. Miller, the subject of this article, is credited with having done more for road racing in South Africa than any other man. In the J2 (opposite) Miller and his passenger put on a great show of weight distribution in a grass track event at Curries Fountain.

drivers' club along the lines of the British Racing Drivers' Club of England formed this stable with a few friends, which operated from a double garage building in Ridge Road, Durban. Foundation members included "Robbie" Martens (Singer Le Mans) and Basil Cook (Singer Le Mans). Others soon joined the fold: Bill King (J2), Tony Starling (M.G.-P single-seater), Mickey Hooper (Talbot), the brothers W. and J. Beattie (Austin 7), Eric Jones, B. Gibb and Bill Ross. Their aim was to have at least one entry in every South African motor race to be run; programmes of the era prove that they succeeded.

On 13 April, the Magna was entered in the first round-the-houses road race in Natal, the Umvoti 50 at Greytown; Les Miller came fourth, having lost ten minutes on the first lap with a visit to the pits, which failed to cure the elusive misfire which continued to trouble him.

The year's motoring ended with the Burman Drive Hill-Climb and Les Miller shared honours with Tony Starling—an article in the *Sunday Tribune* described Miller and Hooper as "fast", safe members of ARDS, showing none of the wildness of other fast men—Starling, for instance, almost slaughtered a section of the crowd when he left the road, ploughed through the turf and put the fear of death into a group of native and Indian hawkers. The air was filled with dust and flying peanuts!!"

The first weeks of 1937 were without doubt the busiest in Les Miller's racing career. On 1 January he was in East London for the third SA Grand Prix. He came a creditable ninth behind the big guns of Europe (Fairfield, Reusch, Rosemeyer and Howe) in a race long to be remembered for the huge Auto-Unions lapping at 119 mph and touching 198 mph down the straight. Tyre problems put paid to their chances.

On 30 January, the Magna was in Johannesburg for the first Rand Grand Prix, but it unfortunately brought Miller to a grinding halt when the steering broke on the eighth lap while he was in the lead. Friday, 26 March, was a happy day for Les—for in the second Umvoti 50

at Greytown he emerged victorious and received from the organizers, the Park Hill Motor Cycle and Light Car Club, his first cheque for £12 10s. (£12.50). He had detuned the Magna before the event by using thick gaskets to drop the compression ratio from double figures and it paid off.

The fourth SA Grand Prix ushered in 1938 and on 1 January Les Miller sped away as limit man—he led for eleven laps before finishing sixth and having endured a really rough ride. On the fourth lap his pneumatic seat cushion punctured and down he went—on to the floorboards. Then oil started to spray from the breather of his extra oil tank, but he held on grimly with oil-saturated gloves. On the last lap he was lying fourth when both Taruffi and Everitt passed him at the post. On 18 April, Miller drove King's J2 to fourth position in the Coronation 100 at Pietermaritz-burg's Alexandra Road Circuit; only eight of thirty-six starters finished.

On Sunday, 21 September 1940, he tied with Starling for first place in the car class at Parkhill MCC Hill-Climb with a net time of 43.4 seconds before going off to serve his country in the South African Air Force as a pilot, as flying was his second great love.

Racing resumed slowly after the war, and with the chronic lack, of new cars and funds that the war years brought, the special builders were soon at it

This interesting line-up of M.G.s is actually the 1937 Arrow Racing Drivers' Stable in front of the group's garages. From left to right we have: Tony Starling (P Type), Val Leslie (J2), Les Miller (L Magna), and Jock Beattie (P Type). Racing in those days required a devotion to the sport plus a combination of driving and mechanical abilities.

102

This stark P Type special is being driven with style by Tony Starling. Several successful specials were developed during the pre- and post-war years as enthusiasts either sought superior performance or modified crashed machinery. Whatever the case, their prime aim was the enjoyment of motorsport to the fullest—and they did!

once again. The Durban M.G. Agents, McCarthy Rodway, had on display in their show-room a TC rolling chassis complete with polished-up engine and transmission. Once it had served its purpose as a static display, it was sold to Miller who set about it in his inimitable way; thus, "Jasper" was born.

In the second Pat Fairfield in 1948, Miller had an outing in Tony Starling's P Type, bringing it home fifth, Beall's ERA winning while the legendary Eddie Hall, then residing in South Africa, finished third in his 4½-litre Bentley. Miller's return to racing was slow. It was only in the latter half of 1949 that he was seriously involved once more, winning the Sydenham Hill-Climb in Durban on 21 November, and coming second on 16 December in the Burman Drive Hill-Climb.

By 1950 he was in the thick of it once more and although he failed to finish the fourth Pat Fairfield Handicap in January (fuel and plug troubles putting an end to a gallant drive) he did finish second to Gordon Henerson in the Senior Coronation at Pietermaritzburg on 10 April. In July Les Miller

journeyed north to Mozambique for the Laurenco Marques Car Races and won the second event. This trophy, the only "foreign" international trophy he ever won, was presented to the Natal Centre at their 1976 *Concours d'Elegance* by Les, a truly wonderful gesture.

The Pat Fairfield Handicap proved to be a hoodoo for Miller, and the fifth event run in January 1951 was no exception; after a great drive, leading for almost the entire race, he dropped out on the second last lap—Harry Pierce won in his own "special", and Frank Brodie finished third. These two drivers were to prove worthy opponents to Miller and many ding-dong Miller–Brodie–Pierce battles ensued, Brodie being the only one to win the SA Drivers Championship, while the luckless Miller had the distinction of being runner-up for three consecutive years. The winner received a Gold Star and on the third ocassion, to commemorate Miller's feat, a special Silver Star was struck for him.

"Spider", the second TC-based special built by Miller, appeared at the Alexandra Park Circuit, Pietermaritzburg, for the Senior Coronation event on Monday, 26 March 1951, bringing Miller home second to Brodie in a closely fought race. In the Junior event run on the previous Saturday, Miller had astounded the crowd with his consistent driving behind the wheel of a locally assembled, supercharged 918 cc side-valve Morris Minor, winning easily to the enthusiastic acclaim of the motoring press. Les Miller then entered the Morris in the East London Winter Handicap, where his original third place was adjusted to sixth on a re-check, so it was back to the single-seaters!

The year 1952 was one of triumph, not only for Les Miller, but also for the "Ecurie" which was to carry his name. In January, three "Ecurie" cars journeyed South to Cape Town for the False Bay 100 at Gunners Circle, Cape Town, Miller coming third behind Stanley Reed in a Citroen special and Le Roux in his CRX Mercury. On 8 March, "Ecurie Miller" returned to Gunners Circle for the Van Riebeeck Trophy Races and this time the 100-mile trip proved to be worth while,

Rushby bringing the trophy back to Durban for the first time. At the Easter Races, oiled plugs once again cost Miller the Senior Coronation Handicap, but "Spider" and Les were proving to be a good combination. The second East London Winter Handicap on Saturday, 21 June, was a huge "Ecurie" success, Miller winning the Barnes Trophy, and Freddie Campbell and Cliff Rushby finishing fifth and ninth. Another "Ecurie" success that year was Freddie Campbell winning the Indian Shield in the hill-climb event at Sydenham.

Les Miller was to repeat his Winter Trophy victory at East London again in 1953 with another great drive on 13 July. All in all it was a good year for "Ecurie Miller", which had grown in strength with the addition of McLean, Pierce Sutcliffe, Hutcheons and Hotchkiss.

Journeying to Cape Town once more for the New Year's Day Handicap staged by the Amateur Automobile Racing Club, Miller won the fifty-mile handicap while Cliff Rushby drove into third place, Campbell's car having

In the Umvoti 50 at Greytown in Natal, Les Miller lays an impressive cloud of dust behind him. That sort of action is called "Bundu-bashing" in South Africa; whatever the name, it looks to be great fun. We'd wager that the M.G. was a particularly capable machine in such action, providing the drivers and spectators with plenty of thrills.

serious overheating problems. The crowd was thrilled by the team's line-astern driving. Miller also entered the main race, the False Bay 100, and finished fourth. However, on 29 January only Freddie Campbell finished the seventh Pat Fairfield race, Miller retiring with oil pressure problems and two other "Ecurie" drivers losing their tail pipes when their flexible exhaust connections broke.

It was, however, in hill-climbs that the "Ecurie Miller" cars made their presence felt. In July it was the Bluff Marine Drive hill-climb, McLean winning and Miller nearly coming to grief in McLean's car, but coming second. At the same venue in August, Miller broke the record with a brilliant run, only 0.5 of a second short of the absolute record held by the super-charged ERA, Hotchkiss and Campbell making it three in a Row. Burman Drive that year was a tragedy as Basil Cook lost his life driving the P Type which Tony Starling's mother had presented to ARDS after Tony had been killed in the Western Desert, and which Cook still entered under that banner. Des Jenkins won the ensuing struggle, Miller coming third.

The inaugural meeting of the Roy Hesketh circuit took place on Saturday, 26 December 1953. Roy Hesketh, a pre-war motorcycle ace and driver of merit, was killed in an air crash early in the war while on active service in the Middle East. 1954 was not the luckiest of years for Miller. Although he won the 1820 Settlers Day event in Durban, and came second to Des Jenkins in the Settlers Handicap at Grand Central, and to Arthur McKenzie's Cooper at Pietermaritzburg (this only by 3 ft), he was to crash at Cape Town. This he did while overtaking team-mate McLean's car at the Van Riebeeck Trophy race on Saturday, 13 March, and although he was only slightly injured his car came off a lot worse. The Ferraris driven by Whitehead and Gaze were not placed. Roddy M. McDowell now joined the stable and at the Centenary Races in October, there were no fewer than six "Ecurie Miller" entries with Les in the latest addition, "Fat Man". Pierce emerged victorious.

"Ecurie Miller" placings in 1955 were McDowell's third in the Fairfield Handicap, Miller's fourth in the Van Riebeeck Trophy, and a fourth, fifth and eighth for Hutcheons, Miller and Campbell in the Easter Golden Jubilee Handicap. For Freddie Campbell this was a sad day, for having been acclaimed and garlanded as the winner, a scoring error was discovered and he was dropped to eighth position. At Burman Drive, fuel starvation robbed Miller of the title, and he came second.

Miller entered fewer events in 1956, coming third to Whitehead and Jennings in the Rand Grand Prix run at Palmietfontein, and likewise behind Fergusson and Jennings in the sixth Winter Handicap. Doug Duff, former SA champion, lost his life in this race in his Sartor special.

Miller came out of retirement to drive in the 1959 Winter Handicap at the invitation of his old friend Max Scheckter, father of future Grand Prix drivers Jody and Ian Scheckter. Max had asked Les to drive a Simca in the production race, and practising in this, plus the fact that he had changed the conventional racing tyres on "Fat Man" to the new and cheaper radials then available (without sponsorship, cost was a major consideration) were regarded as responsible for Miller's crash, ending his racing career and hospitalizing him for five months. A tribute in the race programme on that day said of Miller: "His name is synonymous with motor racing in East London. He has probably done more than any other driver to foster motor racing in South Africa."

When in East London, the "Ecurie Miller" cars were housed in the Scheckter garage, and Max's sons were an accepted part of the feverish pre-race activity, asking questions and showing an almost idolatry interest in Les and the cars. These young prodigies to Miller have both proved to be first-class drivers in their own right, and with Ian joining Jody on the race tracks of the world this coming year, their "Ecurie Miller" spirit could yet give Miller a hand in winning the ultimate trophy. Who knows?

Norman Ewing

106

PEOPLE AND PLACES: A WORLD WIDE ROUNDUP

The young lady and the gentlemen to the left of this column have more than just a youthful outlook on life in common; they are fascinated with the world of M.G., and that includes the cars and the people connected with them. This attraction for the octagon combined with the unusual friendliness of the people in the hobby has led to what is probably the firmest and largest club movement in the world. The largest club is the M.G. Car Club and its president, Captain George E. T. Eyston, in the gentleman to the left; the young girl was seen at the MGCC's 1976 Silverstone race meeting, while Captain Eyston is pictured addressing the 1976 June Gathering of the Faithful of The New England M.G. T Register which took place at Buck Hill Falls in Pennsylvania.

Major meetings for M.G. enthusiasts are held all over the world. On the following few pages we bring you some photographs from some of these meetings. From the States we see views of the Register's two GOFs as well as the New Hope Show and the Bi-Centennial Rally of the Colonial Capitals. Other USA meetings include the GOF South and West, which are very popular. England, of course, abounds in interesting M.G. activities. As a firm tradition, Silverstone is always the highlight. That event includes exciting wheel-to-wheel racing for M.G.s of all vintages as well as a *concours* and driving tests. The friendliness of Silverstone is heightened by the unusual international flavour present as members come from all over for the fun. The premier international mecca for M.G. buffs in 1976 had to be Hausach.

What follows can only be a representation of what the excitement of club membership can mean. Space limitation precludes coverage for every meeting, but we hope that the general atmosphere is communicated. Future annuals will give similar coverage to meetings held at different venues. I encourage event chairmen to send one or two outstanding, captioned, black and white photos to me by 1 November (address in the introduction) so that it will be possible for this section to be more representative.

On the facing page (top) are the finishers of
The New England M.G. T Register's
Bicentennial Rally of the Colonial Capitals.
This hardy group covered almost 2000 miles
in a week driving cars which ranged from an
M Type to an MGB. A TC from Syracuse,
New York, won. The prize? The 1,000,000th
car built at Abingdon and they're all grouped
around it. The TD (bottom) is on course and
fully loaded. The two Red Coats (top) may
be looking for a checkpoint. They're really
Lou Zuger and Al Moss who came in third in
a TC. Almost every night someone's engine
came apart, and Al Moss (bottom) got his
hands dirtier than most.

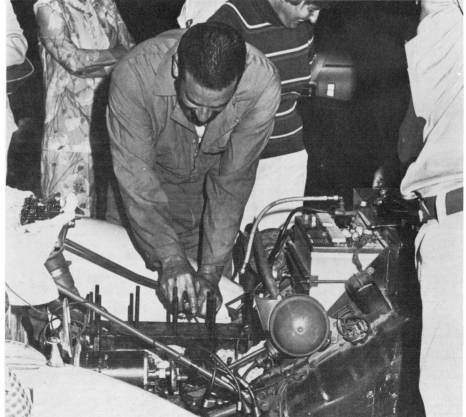

Guess who won! Bryan Wladis and George Cookson are justifiably happy at the announcement that they had won the rally and the grand prize donated by British Leyland of Leonia, New Jersey. As a point of interest, the TC they drove had won the Best TC award at the Register's Buck Hill Gathering of the Faithful the previous month.

Hank Rippert (top) displays grand form flagging in the Germano TC at the finish in Philadelphia. Interestingly enough, that TC logged exactly 1776 miles on the Bicentennial Rally—a happy and unusual coincidence. Presenting the keys to the winners (bottom) is John Dugdale of British Leyland. Mr. Dugdale has a long association with M.G. which goes back to building and racing a special single-seater N Type in the thirties.

The group of M.G.s in the facing page (top) are part of the Premier Class at the Buck Hill GOF of the New England M.G. T Register. These are some of America's finest T Types. A contrast in size (bottom) was caught at the Eagle Bay GOF of the same group. On this page (top) a group of enthusiasts are about to depart New York for a visit to England. Everyone enjoys travelling to England for M.G.C.C. events such as Silverstone (bottom) with its exciting racing.

Silverstone is also the site of an outstanding concours event (top). Another major European event takes place at Zandvoort (bottom) in Holland. Driving up from Switzerland were Mr. and Mrs. Max Zingg. The variety of cars entered (facing page, top) prove the popularity of the Zandvoort meeting. Another attraction. however, was that the Dutch gathering led naturally to the International Rally at Hausach in Germany. The happy group (bottom) are typical of the Hausach spirit.

Three VAs from Germany, Switzerland and England converge on Hausach (top, facing page). Syd Beer's R Type (bottom) was of great interest. On this page, the driving test (top) was full of interesting inventions of the genial host, Gerhard Maier. Located in the Black Forest, there is no lack of beautiful countryside (bottom) and exciting roads for M.G. touring. The TA Tickford (overleaf) is pictured in a beautiful spot.

HOLLAND: BRITAIN'S BRIDGE TO HAUSACH

In 1976 the M.G. Car Club, intending to go to Hausach in huge numbers, planned another trip through Holland. Starting on Saturday, 24 July, the British arrived in two big groups: one in the very early morning in Flushing, in the deep south of the country (the Olau Line from Sheerness to Flushing being one of the shortest and cheapest connections between the UK and the Continent), the second arriving in the late afternoon at the Hook of Holland. Both parties were met at the boats and escorted to Zandvoort. The morning party had to make quite a long trip but was able to avoid heavy traffic. The afternoon was different because the party had to cross The Hague during the rush-hour. The Federation, however, had asked the city police to await the long cavalcade of cars at the entrance of the city and to guide them through. The police performed miracles. They escorted us with their fast motorcycles, using radios, light signals and whistles; they had us drive side-by-side in order to shorten the line of M.G.s.

Zandvoort was a huge success, and the organization under Rob Verhorst was flawless. His dozens of helpers did a magnificent job. Every possible type of M.G. was taking part in the proceedings, which consisted of four driving tests, a parade of cars around the track, and a "clock race" of four laps. In the evening there was a nice party with some music, prize-giving, and much Dutch beer at the circuit restaurant. On Monday morning the party left for Luxembourg.

The trip through Luxembourg included a stop at the *Camping Romantique* near Vianden, where Tom Maathuis, president of the Centre there, had organized a 100-km tour through the most beautiful parts of that country. After that he invited the entire group to a pig roast in the big garden behind his farm. Twenty-one cars were parked inside with another twenty-four outside. From there the British went on to Hausach, arriving on Friday. The Federation of Dutch M.G. Clubs was happy to form a kind of M.G. bridge between Great Britain and the Black Forest.

Rolf ten Kate

THE LAST OF THE TWIN CAMS

Mike Ellman-Brown has owned an impressive array of M.G.s during his lifetime. Some of them are pictured here. The Midget (on the left) was custom-built by Mike and made a very attractive car. The Twin Cam is next in line followed by his Mark II TD and PB.

This is the story of an individual and a car, myself and YD1/2611, the last MGA Twin Cam to be built. Like most stories, however, it does not begin and end there.

To understand how it all started one must go back to the beginning when as a small boy I was mad about cars. When my mother commissioned a miniature of her little horror, the artist insisted on putting two cars in the painting as they had never known a boy so keen on cars. My mother, for instance, frequently conducted her young family in an open Sunbeam in the twenties; by the time I came along, a supertuned Riley was the form together with a close-coupled Packard. After a series of Rileys, this

line was replaced by a Bentley, and one of my most vivid early memories was of this car arriving, for out of it got three men wearing bowler hats—something I had never seen before. It appears that the sales staff of Bentley Motors in those days dressed that way when demonstrating cars, and they had come down to see if it would fit the garage normally occupied by the Riley. This car became a great favourite of my father's; he had it for more than fifteen years and this probably explains my great love for these cars, besides M.G.s, of course. My first driving experience, if you can call it such, was on my mother's knee at the tender age of seven steering a company Vauxhall 10 at the start of

119

World War II and culminating in my backing this car into a post.

During the war there was not much opportunity to indulge in car activities, but immediately after I recommenced by getting the cars out of the garage for my parents and a few secret forays on the road with my mother. When I was finally able to have a licence, I was let loose in the family Morris 8 and later a Morris Minor; economy was the watchword in those days of petrol restrictions. This lasted about a year until I was in the services, where I had a series of motorbikes. With each successive change, the capacity doubled until I decided that if I went on like this I would be in a box 6 ft under. While one of my bikes was off

the road, I was picked up while hitchhiking by a chap in a TD. He was a keen competition driver, and I received a demonstration of driving the like of which I'd not experienced before—Harry Flatters had nothing on him. This impressive demonstration plus the opportunity to study a very nice P Type at camp convinced me that my first car would be an M.G. After a little bit of searching, I came across a very nice 1949 TC in Woodland Green. This car put up with all sorts of punishment. It was tremendous fun and it took me through many adventures. After 10,000 miles I decided it would be prudent to make a change; not wishing my parents to know that I was blowing all my money

In the article Mike discusses his trip to Ireland with his TD in 1955. While there he saw the Twin Cam debut in the TT. He also had a chance to enjoy some pleasant TD motoring.

on cars, I purchased a Woodland Green TD, took the bumpers off, and nobody at home noticed the difference.

This car stayed with me longer and amongst other things it was taken on a three-month sojourn to Ireland in 1955 where I was training. In those days there were no speed limits; what fun I had. We also went to see the 1955 TT, the first appearance of the MGA Twin Cam (rather inglorious, unfortunately), and afterwards I drove around the course. Shortly after this trip I decided it was time for a change, so the TD gave way to a TF, a car which I liked immensely. It was completely stripped down and resprayed in Woodland Green. A series of mechanical disappointments mostly

caused by my local garage's lack of knowledge made me decide, with a certain amount of parental pressure, that perhaps a new M.G. would be a better proposition. As with the TF, the MGA was not available in Woodland Green, so the new car was ordered in black with green interior. I felt that a black engine compartment and boot would look better than bright green, the other alternative. After waiting four weeks it was collected from the factory stripped down, and resprayed in Woodland Green prior to being registered.

What should have been a joyous occasion was really rather a sad one as it meant farewell to the TF. My feeling of loss was heightened when a series of

minor misfortunes culminating in trouble with the new paintwork made me begin to hate my new acquisition. Having just sold a rather expensive camera and beginning to despair with the MGA, I purchased a very smart TA—in Woodland Green—but this was short-lived as a TB Tickford came up and was exchanged for it. The TB was more practical and a super car in every way. This provided everyday transport and allowed me to turn my attention to sorting out the MGA. This accomplished, I embarked upon a busy competition programme of rallies, hill-climbs, and sprints in which, I am pleased to say, I enjoyed a modest degree of success thanks to Michael Hall, my very competent navigator. Occasionally the TB was thrown into battle, but this was not the best car to read a map in so I decided to replace it with another TD. Eventually the most beautiful Woodland Green TD3 Mark II turned up with beige trim which was far too good to use as every-day transport but too good to miss. I could not resist the temptation, however. It was this car which started me off, inspired I might add by Peter Hampton's beautiful collection of Bugattis, on gathering M.G.s together. There followed a supercharged TA with a very special one-off Park Ward body (which I still own) and more mundane M, J and P Types. The PB was also supercharged and this, in turn, led to some more competition with a friend, Rob Davis, driving.

The MGA by this time was no longer pristine after its competition activity, and I decided if I was going to have an MGA in the stable long term it would be prudent to replace it with a new one. The Twin Cam seemed much more collectable apart from being aesthetic-ally more pleasing, so the MGA was traded in September 1959 against the delivery of a Twin Cam in the following spring. In January, however, I heard rumours that the Twin Cam had been discontinued for export and home deliveries were difficult. I wrote to John Thornley, M.G.'s Managing Director, to ask if it was still possible to obtain delivery in the spring. I was pleased to hear that I could. A little later, Mel Jones, a good friend who was with University Motors, was competing in the M.G.C.C. April Rally and while at the half-way control located at the works he fell into conversation with an employee there. He stated that the last Twin Cams were going down the line the next week. I therefore promptly dispatched a letter to John Thornley giving him the speci-fications of the Twin Cam I hoped to obtain. I particularly wanted Woodland Green paintwork which was unofficially obtainable to special order as no green was listed at this time. (I know of four MGAs so finished by the factory about this period.) There followed a fort-night of silence which I could bear no longer, so I wrote to John again asking if I could come and see him as agreed in

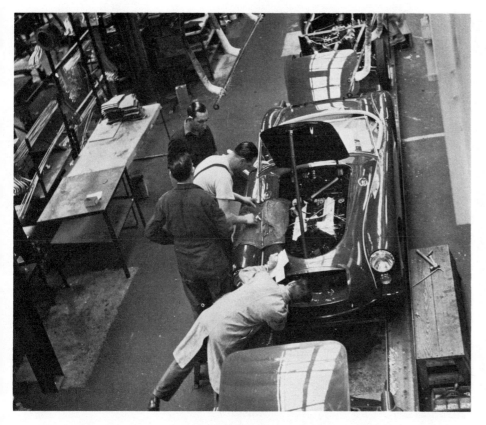

an earlier letter. He replied: "I have been distinctly worried since receiving your letter of 8 April and I do not know quite what to say.

"I think in all the circumstances that it would be a good thing if you could come down to see me and Friday, 29 April which you suggest is quite satisfactory. Unfortunately, I already have a luncheon appointment on that day but will keep the whole afternoon for you."

When we met, John confirmed my worst fears. He told me he had hoped to adjust the specification on one of the last cars to suit my requirements but didn't realize how important the colour was to me. "I don't know what I can do about this, but get your dealer to put in an order and I'll see what I can do," he said. I left Abingdon fearing that the bureaucratic regime controlling the works from Longbridge wouldn't really allow for such favours. Once home I placed an order with Parade Motors in Mitcham and a week later John Smith telephoned to say that the order had been accepted. I really didn't know whether to believe my good fortune or not. Immediately I phoned Mel Jones at University Motors to thank him for his interest and the information that had helped so much. He then suggested that as this would be the only Twin Cam going down the line why not try to obtain photographs of it. I thought this a wonderful idea and contacted Wilson McComb to see if he thought the factory would allow it. He said to leave it to him, and the result is what you see on these pages. Stuart Seager was the photographer to whom I am grateful.

Finally, on 14 June 1960, I went to Abingdon with John Smith to collect the car. I could not have been more proud for there can be few people who have had a car specially made for them by a large manufacturer after production has ceased. To John Thornley who made this all possible, I shall be eternally grateful, for it is one of those things which, as time passes, gives me more and more pleasure. Knowing that the car was for keeps it has been used, frugally, and it has become a true collector's item in more than one sense.

Mike Ellman-Brown

PERSONALITY PROFILE: GORDON COBBAN

Gordon and Elsie Cobban at speed in their new 1953 YB. This was their first M.G. Obtained from the Mill Garage, the idea of competing with it came from Dick Jacobs. This event was the Brighton Rally; the special stage here was at Goodwood.

One doesn't get to become the General Secretary of the M.G. Car Club without a considerable amount of experience with M.G.s. So it is with the present General Secretary, Gordon Cobban. Born in London, he later apprenticed as a carpenter and joiner; while developing those skills, he also acquired a keen business sense which has resulted in his own building contracting business which is capable of handling major projects such as public works contracts. While he was busily engaged in helping his business prosper, he became actively involved with M.G.s and the M.G. Car Club and, thus, doubly busy.

His interest in M.G.s goes back to an Austin 7. It seems that he used one for daily transport in the early fifties and while on the way to work one day he had a puncture. After trying unsuccessfully to locate a garage to repair it promptly, he drove into the well-known Mill Garage. There things were different. Not only did he receive some efficient service, but he also met the friendly and enthusiastic owner, one Dick Jacobs. It didn't take long for a friendship to develop; subsequently, Gordon purchased his first M.G., a YB, from the Mill Garage. Following the YB came a series of M.G.s which were used for daily transport and active competition; these included a 1954 TF, 1956 MGA, ZB, two 1300s, and a GT. Gordon relied on Dick Jacobs for maintenance

A classic scene on the 1955 Land's End Trial. The TF replaced the YB and was used in a variety of events. Gordon recalls regularly beating Bill Constable's TD with it. Bill bought the TF when Gordon acquired his MGA and sold his TD to Peter Tomei, who promptly turned the tables by using it to beat Bill in the TF.

and advice, especially during those seasons in which he actively competed. Over the years Gordon has participated in many national and international rallies, trials, and considerable club racing on England's various circuits.

Often navigating for him on those early rallies was his friendly wife, Elsie. No mention of Gordon and his relationship with M.G. Car Club is complete without Elsie, for she is always there doing something most important to make sure things go smoothly. Whether it be standing in the lonely, cold press room at Silverstone handing out results and answering a million questions, or baking in the blazing sun at Beaulieu signing-up new members, Elsie is

always there working for the club and keeping people happy.

Gordon joined the M.G. Car Club in 1953 after Dick Jacobs had encouraged him to enter the club races at Silverstone. Even in those days, one had to be a member in order to enter. Yes, even Gordon Cobban had to show his membership card in order to enter races and events, and the practice has never changed—no card, no entry. On joining Gordon became a member of the South East Centre as well. This has always been a very active Centre and they welcomed Gordon and Elsie to their events. By 1955 he was on their committee and in 1958 became the Centre's secretary. In 1969 he succeeded

Wilson McComb as the main club's General Secretary on the occasion of the club's independence from the parent firm. Up to that time, the M.G.C.C. had received varying degrees of support from the firm and felt secure with that sort of backing. With the major shake-up of the whole Leyland organization came a decision to let the clubs go it alone. This might have meant the end for a club with less spirit and dedication, but for the M.G.C.C. it was a challenge which they met squarely and conquered. Gordon sees this independence as a distinct plus factor: "We are masters of our own destiny," he says and points to the sustained membership and the member awareness

and dedication to succeed on its own. Without the company's support, more volunteers have been necessary to accomplish all of the tasks to make the club function, thus more members than ever are involved. As the General Secretary, Gordon sees himself as trying to keep everyone happy; that is the ideal, but it is, of course, an impossible task. Primarily he is responsible for the business side of the club. Always looking to the President and Chairman for guidance, he finds that in the end he must be a combination businessman, accountant and lawyer. It's not an easy job, but it has its rewards which may be summed up in his feelings towards his seventeen-year stint as Clerk of the

The MGA at the Bugatti Owner's Club Sixth Annual Speed Hill-Climb at Prescott in 1957. Gordon enjoyed competing with the MGA and even drove a University Motors car in the RAC International Rally. The car was placed third at the half-way point but an error on the last half put them out of the trophies.

Course for the Silverstone meeting, the club's main event each year. Gordon stated that the pressures of dealing with the many details and problems which come up during the course of that weekend do make him tense. Further, he knows that there will come a moment sometime during the event when he'll think, "Never again". But when it's all over and he reflects on the pleasures of working with such an efficient and dedicated group of marshals and officials, then the satisfaction of that makes it all worth while.

Gordon sees the club going on for years regardless of the future of the marque. Collectable cars will always need a club structure to cater for their unique problems. The various Registers of the M.G. Car Club are set up to do exactly this.

In addition to a successful business and the M.G.C.C. to occupy his time, Gordon is also an active Rotarian. In the States we say that if you want something done, ask a busy person to do it; Gordon Cobban is living proof of this.

The MGA (top) in the National Six-Hour Relay Race at Silverstone in 1958. At a hill-climb site (bottom) we have a typical view of Gordon and Elsie. Their concern for good organization is important to the success of many meetings.

The Supreme British
Sports Car

The M.G. Midget Mark II. Montlhéry Model

The M.G. Car Company Ltd.
Abingdon-on-Thames

The M.G. Midget Mark II
Montlhery Model

The fastest and finest 750 c.c. car money can buy.

CHASSIS DIMENSIONS.

Number of cylinders—4.
Bore and stroke—57 mm. by 73 mm. (746 c.c.).
Treasury rating—8.05 (Tax £8.).
Track—3 ft. 6 in.
Wheelbase—6 ft. 9 in.
Overall width 4 ft. 4¼ in.
Overall length—11 ft. 4 in.
Overall height—Hood up, 4 ft. 4¾ in. ; Hood down, 3 ft. 8 in.
Petrol tank capacity—15 gals.
Maximum ground clearance—6½ in.

ENGINE.—Four cylinders cast on block. Exceptionally sturdy two-bearing counter-balanced crankshaft. Overhead valves operated through fingers by overhead camshaft carried on detachable cylinder head. Aluminium pistons with special steel connecting rods.

GEARBOX.—Four speed latest advanced design of the twin top type. Bottom gear of the low emergency order, whilst the second, third and top are of the close ratio variety specially selected for high speed performance. The gearbox ratios are as follows :—

Top	-	1—1.
Third	-	1.37—1.
Second	-	2—1.
First	-	4.01—1.
Reverse	-	4.01—1.

LUBRICATION.—Engine. The engine is pressure lubricated throughout by a gear type pump. Oil is carried in a large Electron sump with cooling fins, having a capacity of one gallon. An automatic float feed device is used to maintain a level of oil in sump from an auxiliary oil tank on the dash, the capacity of the dash tank is 15 pints.

Chassis. Chassis lubrication is by means of Tecalemit grease gun, grouped nipples being used together with the necessary pipes in all places where the connections would otherwise be inaccessible.

CARBURETTER.—The standard carburetter is a large S.U. down-draft fitted to a special down-draft manifold with an exhaust heated hot spot immediately below the carburetter outlet.

COOLING.—The cooling is by syphon circulation from the engine to the radiator in the case of the unsupercharged models. Where a supercharger is fitted a pump driven low down at the front end of the engine is incorporated at standard. The radiator is of the film type with a chromium plated brass shell of exclusive M.G. design.

TRANSMISSION.—A two-plate dry clutch is used in conjunction with the four speed gearbox and engine unit. The propeller shaft is of the Hardy Spicer type with all metal universal joints, whilst the back axle is of straight forward design with the usual final bevel drive, having a ratio of 5.37 to 1.

CHASSIS FRAME.—This is of special underslung design, the floor line being only 11 in. from the ground. The frame is built with tubular cross members and has a steel tube cross brace at the rear end, the design as a whole being an ideal combination of stiffness under normal conditions and ability to yield to heavy blows without injury. The low build gives remarkable road holding.

SPRINGS.—These are flat and underslung both front and rear, all the springs are anchored at the front end and mounted in a slide at the rear end, there being a maximum of resistance to any transverse movement or oscillation. In accordance with racing practice the springs are taped and bound with cord.

STEERING.—This is of normal type with transverse draglink. A spring spoke steering wheel is fitted. The steering is very light and yet absolutely positive at any speed at which the car can be driven.

BRAKES.—A special brake gear is used, all four brakes being operated by both the foot pedal and the hand brake lever. The brakes are operated by Bowden cables in such a way that axle

The M.G. Midget Mark II

Montlhery Model—*continued*

movements are not communicated to the brake pedal even on the roughest roads. The hand brake lever is of racing type with a press down ratchet which only locks it when required so that the hand brake can be used continuously if desired without any interference from the ratchet. Rapid adjustments are provided for both foot brake and hand brake. It is possible to adjust the brakes while driving if necessary, but actually the brakes have a very long life, and adjustment normally is seldom required.

ELECTRICAL.—The Rotax 6 volt set is used incorporating separate dynamo and starter with a large capacity battery. Two headlamps, two side lamps and a tail lamp are supplied. In addition to this two separate ignition coils are provided with a change-over switch as part of the standard equipment. Every circuit on the car is wired and fused separately and the fuse box is readily accessible at the back of the forward bulk head which is exposed when the bonnet is lifted.

SILENCING ARRANGEMENTS.—An expansion chamber, tail pipe and fish tail conforming to the Brooklands silencer regulations are fitted as standard. As the degree of silence provided by this arrangement is possibly insufficient for ordinary road use a special detachable internal silencing tube is fitted, which can readily be removed for racing purposes.

PETROL.—The fuel is carried in a large capacity tank at the rear end and is fed to the carburetters by means of two electric fuel pumps. Number two pump can empty the whole tank, but number one pump cannot pump out the last two gallons, so that by running normally on number one pump the reserve supply is always available by switching on number two.

FILLERS.—A quick acting filler cap is provided for the petrol tank.

WHEELS.—Rudge-Whitworth wheels of racing design are supplied, these are hub detachable, not the cheaper stud type. A spare wheel is supplied and carried in the tail. Dunlop tyres to fit the 19 by 3½ rims are supplied as standard.

SHOCK ABSORBERS.—Hartford shock absorbers are supplied as standard, the rear shock absorbers being of a special transverse type. The new remote telecontrol adjustment is fitted to the rear shock absorbers the control being mounted above the steering column.

INSTRUMENTS.—The standard instruments are as follows :— 6 in. Jaegar revolution counter, oil pressure gauge, oil thermometer, petrol gauge, oil tank gauge, ammeter, 8-day clock, ignition tell-tale and the following switches :—Fuel pump 1, fuel pump 2, ignition switch, side and tail lamp switch, nearside headlamp switch, and offside headlamp switch. The carburetter jet control, starting button and the air pump for the oil tank gauge are also mounted on the facia board.

SPECIAL EQUIPMENT.—The engines are supplied as standard with medium compression pistons, for actual racing work high compression pistons can be supplied. With a supercharger or high compression pistons fitted, it is necessary to add that the engine guarantee is definitely withdrawn, as considerable damage can result by lack of discretion on the part of the driver, over which we have no control.

TYRES.—The standard tyres supplied are 27 in. by 4 in. Dunlop Fort tyres of normal pattern. While these tyres are ideal for ordinary use, special tyres of racing pattern to withstand extreme heat are supplied by the Dunlop Company to fit the same rims. These special racing tyres can only be supplied for an actual race and are not recommended for ordinary road work, for which the standard tyre is actually more suitable.

SUPERCHARGING.—The Montlhery Midget is specially adapted for supercharging, complete supercharger equipment being supplied at an extra cost.

SUPERCHARGER.—The supercharger used is a number 7 Power plus with reduction gear, the supercharger running at approximately three-quarters engine speed. The supercharger is mounted at the front end of the crankshaft and driven by a special coupling shaft with all metal universal joints so arranged that no end thrust can be communicated to the blower drive. A special twin inlet pipe is used (M.G. patent pending) together with a double throttle control which ensures quick acceleration, even from the lowest speeds. The whole supercharger assembly is enclosed in a neat front fairing which is readily detachable for inspection purposes.

CARBURETTERS.—The carburetter used is a special type S.U. with horizontal piston.

COACHWORK.—The Montlhery M.G. Midget Mark II model is sold only as a complete two-seater with a panelled body conforming to the usual road-racing regulations. The upholstery is in real leather, and the bucket seats have ample adjustment to accommodate the tallest driver in comfort. A Triplex Glass Windscreen which folds flat forward on the scuttle, is fitted as standard, but for competition purposes a gauze screen can be fitted. The car is finished in British Racing Green with upholstery to match, but colours to choice may be had at an extra charge (see list of extras).

LIST OF EXTRAS.

Chronograph clock	£7 7 0	fitted.
Speedometer (mounted on bracket) ...	£5 6 0	,,
Wire gauze racing screen	£9 0 0	
Quick acting filler cap for radiator ...	£2 5 0	
Supercharger, water pump and all drive parts	£85 0 0	
Extra for colour exterior and upholstery ...	£10 0 0	
Conversion of existing unsupercharged car including supply of supercharger, special induction pipe, blow off valve, all drive parts, water pump and fitting	£100 0 0	

Prices: Supercharged - £575
Unsupercharged - £490

The right is reserved to vary this specification without notice.

The Montlhery Midget's Magnificent Marque
1931

The first 750 c.c. car to exceed 100 m.p.h.
The first 750 c.c. car to cover 100 miles in one hour

Double-Twelve Hour Race, 1930.
Team Prize.

Double-Twelve Hour Race, 1931.
First Five Places in Race.
First Five Places in Class H.
Team Prize.

Irish Grand Prix., 1931.
First, Third and Fourth winning Phœnix Trophy.
First, Second and Third in First Day's Race winning Soarstat Cup.
R.I.A.C. Trophy.
Wakefield Trophy.

The Ulster T.T., 1931.
First and Third in Race.

German Grand Prix, 1931.
First car under 750 c.c.
    (entered by Capt. F. H. B. Samuelson).

Shelsley Walsh, 1931.
First Class " H " Sports.
First Class " H " Racing.
International Race Cup.

500 Mile Race.
Third at 92.17 m.p.h.
Fifth at 89.82 m.p.h.
Team Prize.
All Class " H " Awards.

Class " H " under 750 cc.
First car to exceed 100 m.p.h.
First car to cover 100 miles in one hour.

Mr. G. E. T. EYSTON in the first 750 c.c. car to exceed 100 m.p.h.

LORD MARCH, the Winner of the Double-Twelve Hour Race

MR. NORMAN BLACK, the Winner of the Irish Grand Prix

The brochure reproduced on the previous
four pages provides many details about
the C Type pictured above. The K3 (overleaf)
shown with Sir William Morris is the car
which won the 1933 Tourist Trophy;
following that photo is the rare sales
brochure for the K3, J4, and J5 racing M.G.s.

THIS IS THE WINNING MG MAGNETTE
Driven by NUVOLARI in the ULSTER T.T.

17

For The Racing Motorist

A detailed description of the J4 and J5 M.G. Midgets and the K3 M.G. Magnette Racing Models

The M.G. Magnette
K3 Racing Model

THE M.G. CAR COMPANY LIMITED, ABINGDON-ON-THAMES, Berkshire
Export Department : **STRATTON HOUSE, 80 PICCADILLY, W.I**

Introduction to the M.G. Midget and the M.G. Magnette Racing Models

TO meet the demand for specially fast editions of the M.G. Midget and the M.G. Magnette for competition work and road racing, the M.G. Midget Model J4 and J5 and the M.G. Magnette K3 have been introduced. The J4 is a supercharged and the J5 an unsupercharged M.G. Midget, and the K3 is a supercharged M.G. Magnette.

The M.G. Midget winning the 1931 J.C.C. Double-Twelve Hours Race

The world-famous 746 c.c. M.G. Midget, which during 1931-2 carried all before it, really needs no introduction; as everyone knows, it made motor racing history by taking during 1931 the first five places and team prize in the Junior Car Club Double-Twelve Hours Race, winning the Irish Grand Prix and Ulster T.T., coming in third in the B.R.D.C. 500 Miles Race, and in the same event winning the team award, and in 1932 finishing third in the J.C.C. 1000 Miles event, the Ulster T.T., and winning outright at 96·17 m.p.h. the B.R.D.C. 500 Miles, the fastest long-distance event in the world.

Its record-breaking career is equally amazing, so numerous have been the successes. It was the first car in the 750 c.c. category to exceed 100 m.p.h., also to achieve the coveted 100 in the hour (from standing start). The highest speed achieved by a car of this size was recorded when a fraction over two miles a minute was attained in December 1932 by the M.G. Midget, which now holds every existing record in its class, an unparalleled achievement.

With this wealth of experience available it follows that very few experimental features will be found in the M.G. Midget Racing Model; this applies also to the M.G. Magnette Racing Model, which follows very closely the general layout and design.

Winning the 1931 Ulster T.T. Race

Page Two

Introduction to the M.G. Midget and the M.G. Magnette
Racing Models—*continued*

With the greater weight and higher speed of the M.G. Magnette it was considered essential that the braking should receive very special attention.

The brakes represent the very latest word, the brake-shoes, back plate and drums being of elektron, the latter with special cast liners with ground inner surfaces—operation is by the well-tried M.G. cased cable system.

The frame, with tubular cross members, is underslung and very rigid, the side members being actually below axle centres.

The six-cylinder M.G. Magnette engine of 1086 c.c. is equipped with B.T.H. polar inductor magneto, and fuel is fed by a large bore carburetter, employing a special M.G. induction system.

The gearbox is of the pre-selective type, a very great asset when racing, since by virtue of the quick changes which can be made, acceleration is increased considerably.

Following M.G. policy, there is not the slightest difference between these new M.G. racing models supplied for that purpose and those sold in the ordinary way for fast touring. The keynote of both models is the acme of controllability at the highest speeds, superlative brakes, powers of acceleration, staying power, and speed that make them worthy opponents in any racing company.

Finishing third and class winner in the J.C.C. 1000 Miles Race

The M.G. Midget J4 Supercharged and J5 Unsupercharged Models

The M.G. Midget J4 Model

Specification

ENGINE. Four-cylinder engine cast en bloc with the upper half of the crank chamber. Exceptionally sturdy two-bearing counterbalanced crankshaft. Overhead valves operated through fingers by overhead camshaft carried on detachable cylinder head, all to special M.G. design, with inlet ports on one side and exhaust ports on the other side to ensure rapid combustion. The latest type 14 mm. sparking plugs have also been adopted. Camshaft drive by spiral bevel gears and vertical shaft at front end of engine, incorporated in this arrangement being the dynamo. Special aluminium pistons with steel connecting rods of particular design are fitted, each piston having three rings. Lubrication of the engine has of necessity received very special consideration. It is, of course, pressure throughout, the circulation being effected by an extra large gear type pump. There is also a Tecalemit 100% oil filter fitted. The oil is carried in a large elektron sump having cooling fins and a capacity of approximately 1 gallon. Fitted to the side of the sump is an automatic float feed device, which is used to maintain a level of oil in the sump from an auxiliary oil tank in the dash, the capacity of the tank being about 15 pints.

GEARBOX. The straightforward gearbox is of the latest advanced design of the twin-top type. Bottom gear of the low emergency order, whilst the second, third and top are of the close ratio variety specially selected for high-speed performance. The gearbox ratios are as follows :—

Top	...	1 —1
Third	...	1.37—1
Second	...	1.86—1
First	...	2.69—1
Reverse	...	2.69—1

GEARBOX (Pre-selective). Under certain conditions of racing when quick gear changes are essential it is a very definite advantage if the car is fitted with a pre-selective gearbox. Therefore we are offering this type of gearbox as an optional fitment for an additional £25 on the racing models. The pre-selective gearbox is manufactured under Wilson patents. Gear change is effected by depressing and releasing the clutch pedal after the gear required has been selected. The change speed lever is mounted on a gearbox extension close handy for the left hand. The gearbox ratios are as follows :—

Top	...	1 —1
Third	...	1.36—1
Second	...	2.0 —1
First	...	3.4 —1
Reverse	...	5.07—1

CARBURETTERS. Two large S.U. semi-downdraught automatic piston type with hand mixture control. When, however, the Powerplus supercharger is fitted, then the carburetter is bolted on to the casing of the supercharger and feeds through the special M.G. induction system to the inlet manifold. This special induction manifold renders the engine extremely tractable at low speeds, without in the slightest interfering with its very large power output, the idea being to maintain the gas velocity by using a small diameter induction pipe when the engine is running with the throttle closed, whilst the larger induction pipe comes in when the throttle is open and the engine is turning over fast.

COOLING. The cooling on both supercharged and unsupercharged models is by a positively driven pump from the crankshaft. The radiator is of the film type with a chromium-plated brass shell of exclusive M.G. design.

TRANSMISSION. When a straightforward type gearbox is fitted, a two-plate dry clutch is used in conjunction with the four-speed gearbox and engine unit. The propeller shaft is of the Hardy Spicer type with all-metal universal joints, whilst the back axle is of straightforward design with straight bevel final drive and ratios to order from standard selection to suit requirements. In the case of the pre-selective gearbox the clutch is incorporated in the gearbox unit.

CHASSIS FRAME. This is of special underslung design, the floor line being only 11 in. from the ground. The frame is built with tubular cross members and has a tubular steel brace at the rear end, the design as a whole being an ideal combination of stiffness under normal conditions and ability to yield to heavy blows without injury. The low build gives remarkable road holding.
The chassis is lubricated by means of a Tecalemit grease gun, grouped nipples being used together with the necessary pipe lines in all places where connections would otherwise be inaccessible.

STEERING. Cam steering is used, whilst the steering column is adjustable for rake, and is fitted with a special racing type spring spoke steering wheel, having a thin rubber-covered rim, the diameter of which is 18 in. The latest M.G. (Patent pending) twin track steering is also incorporated.

SPRINGS. These are flat and underslung, both front and rear. All springs are anchored at the front end and mounted in a slide at the rear end, there being a maximum of resistance to any transverse movement or oscillation. In accordance with racing practice the springs are taped and bound with cord.

BRAKES. A special brake gear is used, all four brakes being operated by both the foot pedal and the hand brake lever. The brakes with 12 in. drums and cooling fins are operated by Bowden cables in such a way that axle movements are not communicated to the brake pedal even on the roughest roads. The hand brake lever is of racing type, with a press-down ratchet which only locks it when required, so that the hand brake can be used continuously if desired without any interference from the ratchet. Rapid adjustments are provided for both foot brake and hand brake. It is possible to adjust the brakes while driving if necessary, but actually the brakes have a very long life, and adjustment normally is seldom required.

ELECTRICAL. A Rotax 12-volt set is used, incorporating separate dynamo and starter with a large capacity battery. Two headlamps, two sidelamps, tail-lamp, dashlamps and electric windscreen wiper are supplied. In addition to this two separate ignition coils are provided. Every circuit on the car is wired and fused separately, and the fusebox is readily accessible.

SILENCING ARRANGEMENTS. An expansion chamber, tail pipe and fish tail conforming to the Brooklands silencer regulations are fitted as standard. As the degree of silence provided by this arrangement is possibly insufficient for ordinary road use, a special detachable internal silencing tube is fitted, which can readily be removed for racing purposes.

PETROL. The fuel is carried in a large capacity tank at the rear end and is fed to the carburetter by means of two electric fuel pumps. Number 2 pump can empty the whole tank, but Number 1 pump cannot pump out the last two gallons, so that by running normally on No. 1 pump the reserve supply is always available by switching on Number 2.

FILLERS. A quick-acting filler cap is provided for the petrol tank and radiator.

WHEELS. Rudge-Whitworth wheels of racing design are supplied. These are hub detachable. A spare wheel is supplied and carried in the tail. Dunlop tyres to fit the 19 in. by 3½ in. rims are supplied as standard.

SHOCK ABSORBERS. Hartford shock absorbers are supplied as standard, the rear shock absorbers being of a special transverse type.

INSTRUMENTS. The standard instruments are as follows :— 6 in. Jaegar revolution counter, oil pressure gauge, oil and water thermometers, petrol gauge, oil tank gauge, ammeter, 8-day clock, ignition tell-tale and the following switches :—Fuel pump 1, fuel pump 2, ignition switch, side and tail-lamp switch, near-side headlamp switch, and off-side headlamp switch. The carburetter jet control, starting button and the air pump for the oil tank gauge are also mounted on the facia board. A full kit of tools is included.

SPECIAL EQUIPMENT. The engines are supplied as standard with medium compression pistons ; for actual racing with unsupercharged cars high compression pistons can be supplied.

TYRES. The standard tyres supplied are 4.50 in. by 19 in. Dunlop Fort tyres of normal pattern. While these tyres are ideal for ordinary use, special tyres of racing pattern to withstand extreme heat are supplied by the Dunlop Company to fit the same rims. These special racing tyres can only be supplied by the makers for an actual race and are not recommended for ordinary road work, for which the standard tyre is actually more suitable.

SUPERCHARGER. The supercharger used is a Number 7 Powerplus with reduction gear, the supercharger running at approximately three-quarters engine speed. The supercharger is mounted at the front end of the crankshaft and driven by a special coupling shaft with all-metal universal joints so arranged that no end thrust can be communicated to the blower drive. A pressure blow-off valve is fitted on the inlet manifold. The whole supercharger assembly is enclosed in a neat front fairing which is readily detachable for inspection purposes.

COACHWORK. The M.G. Midget J4 and J5 models are offered as chassis complete with lamps, instruments, all electrical equipment and a neat set of tools, but without wings, wing stays or bonnet, for those who desire to have their own special type of bodies built thereon. They are also offered as complete two-seaters with panelled bodywork, conforming to the usual road racing regulations. A special detachable tail is available for streamlining the Ulster bodies. The upholstery is in real leather and the bucket seats have ample adjustment. A Triplex glass windscreen, which folds flat forward on the scuttle, is fitted as standard, but under certain racing conditions where it is inadvisable to carry a glass screen, a gauze screen can be fitted as an extra. The standard finish is British Racing Green with upholstery to match, but any of the range of M.G. special colours can be had at no additional charge.

LIST OF EXTRAS. Chronograph clock £7 7s. fitted. Speedometer (mounted on bracket) £5 6s. fitted. Wire gauze racing screen £9. Conversion of existing unsupercharged car, including supply of supercharger, special induction pipe, blow-off valve, all drive parts, water pump and fitting, £100.
The special M.G. colours are :—

Ulster Green/Dublin Green	Abingdon Grey/Brooklands Grey
Light Fawn/Old Ivory	Saratoga Red/Carmine Red
Cambridge Blue/Oxford Blue	Ebony Black/White
	No Charge.

Any special colours other than the above, £4 10s.
Any deviation from any one of the five following standard leathers :—Apple Green, Tudor Brown, Deep Red, Cerulean Blue, Suede Grey leather, £5 5s.
Extra for No. 8 Powerplus supercharger in place of No. 7, £12.

PRICES.

Chassis J4 with straightforward type gearbox	}	
Ditto with close ratio pre-selective type gearbox	} Chassis	
Chassis J5 with straightforward type gearbox	} prices on	
Ditto with pre-selective type gearbox ...	} application	
Two-seater. J4 T.T. coachwork, with straightforward gearbox...		£445
Ditto with pre-selective close ratio racing type gearbox		£480
Two-seater. J5 T.T. coachwork, with straightforward gearbox...		£395
Ditto with pre-selective close ratio racing type gearbox		£430
Detachable streamlined tail...		£35

The right is reserved to vary this specification without notice.

The M.G. Magnette K3 Racing Model
(Supercharged)

The M.G. Magnette K3 Supercharged Racing Model

Specification

ENGINE. 1086 c.c. 6-cylinder engine, bore 57 mm., stroke 71 mm., cast en bloc with the upper half of the crank chamber. Exceptionally sturdy four-bearing balanced crankshaft machined all over. Overhead valves of special heat-resisting steel alloy with triple springs are operated through fingers by overhead camshaft carried on detachable cylinder head, all to special M.G. design. The inlet ports are on the one side of the head and the exhaust on the other, each having six separate ports. Camshaft drive is by spiral bevel gears and vertical shaft at the front end of the engine, incorporated in this arrangement being the dynamo. Special aluminium pistons with steel connecting rods of particular design are fitted, each piston having three rings. Plugs are the latest 14 mm. type.

Lubrication of the engine has of necessity received very special consideration. It is, of course, pressure throughout, the circulation being effected by an extra large gear type pump which feeds the oil through a filter situated between the pump and the feed to the main and big-end bearings. The oil is carried in a large elektron sump, having cooling fins and a capacity of approximately 1¾ gallons. Fitted to the side of the sump is an automatic float feed device, which is used to maintain a level of oil in the sump from an auxiliary oil tank in the dash, the capacity of the tank being about 15 pints.

CARBURETTER. A large size S.U. automatic type carburetter is bolted on to the casing of the supercharger with suitable gauze over the air intake. A "Ki-gass" fuel spray is fitted to assist starting. Feed is through a special M.G. induction system to the inlet manifold.

SUPERCHARGER. The M.G. Magnette model K3 is supplied as standard with a supercharger. The type used is a Powerplus No. 9, of eccentric vane type with reduction gear, the supercharger running at approximately three-quarters engine speed. The supercharger is mounted at the front end of the crankshaft and driven by a special coupling shaft with all-metal universal joints so arranged that no end thrust can be communicated to the blower drive. Lubrication of the supercharger bearings is at low pressure from the cylinder head. The whole assembly is enclosed in a neat front fairing which is readily detachable for inspection purposes.

GEARBOX (Pre-selective). Either a pre-selective gearbox (Wilson patent) or a straightforward 4-speed type is available on the racing M.G. Magnette models. With the pre-selective type of gearbox the gear is selected by means of a central lever mounted on extension of the gearbox top in a positive gate with reverse stop, the actual change after pre-selecting the gear being performed automatically by depressing the clutch pedal. A new and ingenious arrangement of brakes on the epicyclic mechanism causes them to operate on a Servo principle,

giving a strong grip when driving and a much weaker grip when the car over-runs the engine. Thus the need for an artificial coupling between the engine and the gearbox is entirely avoided. Very quick changes can be made and acceleration and deceleration are very greatly improved. The gearbox ratios are as follows, final ratios being dependent on the back axle ratio selected :—

Top	... ...	1 —1
Third	... ...	1.36—1
Second	... ...	2.0 —1
First	... ...	3.4 —1
Reverse	... ...	5.07—1

GEARBOX (Straightforward type). The straightforward gearbox for this model is of the close ratio 4-speed pattern with central remote control brought close up to the left hand on an extension of the gearbox. The gear ratios are as follows :—

Top	... ...	1 —1
Third	... ...	1.37—1
Second	... ...	1.86—1
First	... ...	2.69—1
Reverse	... ...	2.69—1

TRANSMISSION. The clutch is incorporated in the gearbox unit when a pre-selective gearbox is fitted, and in the case of a straightforward box a two-plate large diameter clutch is standard. The propeller shaft is of the Hardy Spicer type with all-metal universal joints, whilst the back axle is of three-quarter floating design with straight bevel final drive, ratio according to back axle selected from standard range to suit particular requirement.

COOLING. Is by pump driven low down at the front end of the engine. The radiator, with quick filler cap, is of the film type of exclusive M.G. design with stoneguard incorporated.

CHASSIS FRAME. This is of special underslung design, the floor line being approximately 12 in. from the ground. The frame is built up with tubular cross members and has a special centre bracing and a tubular steel brace at the rear end, the design as a whole being a compromise of stiffness under normal conditions and the ability to yield to heavy blows without injury. The chassis is lubricated by Tecalemit grease gun, grouped nipples being used, together with the necessary pipe line in all places where connections would otherwise be inaccessible.

SPRINGS. These are half-elliptic and flat under load, being underslung both front and rear; all springs are anchored at the front end and mounted in a slide at the rear end, there being a maximum of resistance to any transverse movement or oscillation. In accordance with racing practice the springs are taped and bound with cord.

BRAKES. Realising the paramount importance of effective braking under modern racing conditions, very special attention has been paid to this feature of the chassis. For the size and weight of the car the brakes are enormous, but in spite of their large diameter, by use of elektron for the shoes, back plate and drums, the latter with suitable cast iron liners, the weight has been kept down to a minimum. All four brakes are operated by either the pedal or the hand brake lever or both. The actual operation is by the special M.G. design of cased cable, which has been largely copied, the feature of this system being that axle movements are not communicated back to the brake pedal, even on the roughest of roads. The diameter of the brake-drums is over 13 in. A special brace is fitted from an extension of the front axle king pins to the chassis side members, to take the strain of applied braking forces from the front axle beam.

The hand brake lever is of the racing type with a press-down ratchet pawl which only locks it when required, so that the hand brake can be used continuously if desired without any interference from the ratchet. Rapid adjustments are provided for both foot and hand brake, and it is possible to adjust the brakes while driving if necessary, but actually they have a very long life and adjustment normally is seldom required.

STEERING. Special cam steering is used, whilst the steering column is adjustable for rake and is fitted with a special racing type spring spoked steering wheel having a thin rubber-covered rim and a diameter of 18 in. The latest M.G. (Patent pending) twin track rod is incorporated which equalises the steering effort and eliminates a good deal of the spring which is present in the straightforward fore and aft draglink types of gear.

ELECTRICAL. A Rotax 12-volt set is used, incorporating separate dynamo and starter, with two separate large capacity 6-volt batteries wired in series for storage; two headlamps,

WHEELS. Rudge-Whitworth wheels of racing design are supplied; these are hub detachable. A spare wheel is supplied and carried at the back. Dunlop tyres to fit the 19 in. by 3½ in. rims are supplied as standard.

SHOCK ABSORBERS. Hartford shock absorbers are supplied as standard, the rear shock absorber being of a special transverse type, four of which are fitted to the rear axle.

TYRES. The standard tyres supplied are 4.50 in. by 19 in. Dunlop Fort tyres of normal pattern. Whilst these tyres are ideal for ordinary use, special tyres of racing pattern to withstand extreme heat are supplied by the Dunlop Company to fit the same rims. These special racing tyres can only be supplied by the makers for an actual race and are not recommended for ordinary road work, for which the standard tyre is actually more suitable.

COACHWORK. The M.G. Magnette K3 model is offered as a chassis, complete with lamps, instruments, all electrical equipment and tools, but without wings, wing stays or bonnet, for those who desire to have their own special type of bodies built thereon. It is also offered as a complete two-seater of the T.T. type as illustrated with a panelled body conforming to the usual road racing regulations, and if desired a detachable streamline tail is available. The upholstery is in real leather and the bucket seats have ample adjustment to accommodate the tallest driver in comfort. A Triplex glass windscreen which folds forward flat on the scuttle is fitted as standard. The exterior finish for the body is British Racing Green, with upholstery to match, but any of the range of M.G. colours may be had if desired for no additional charge.

by running normally on Number 1 pump the reserve supply is always available by switching on Number 2.

Two quick-acting filler caps are provided for the petrol tank.

The M.G. Magnette Racing Model

Rear view of M.G. Magnette Racing model with T.T. Coachwork

two sidelamps, tail-lamp, dashlamps and electric windscreen wiper are supplied. Ignition is by polar inductor magneto of proved reliability. Every circuit on the car is wired and fused separately and the fusebox is mounted on the near-side of the dash.

INSTRUMENTS. The standard instruments are as follows :— 6 in. Jaegar revolution counter, oil pressure gauge, oil and water thermometers, petrol gauge, oil tank gauge, ammeter, supercharger pressure gauge, 8-day clock, and the following switches :—Fuel pump 1, fuel pump 2, ignition switch, side and tail switch, near-side headlamp switch and off-side headlamp switch. Two electric horns with synchronised notes are standard. Starter button and the air pump for the oil tank gauge and "Ki-gass" control are also mounted on the facia board.

SILENCING ARRANGEMENTS. An outside exhaust system with a separate branch for each port is fitted, and an expansion chamber, tail pipe and fish tail conforming with the Brooklands silencing regulations are fitted as standard. As the degree of silence provided by this arrangement is possibly insufficient for ordinary road use, a special detachable internal silencing tube is fitted which can readily be removed for racing purposes.

PETROL. The fuel is carried in a 23-gallon tank at the rear end and is fed to the carburetters by means of two electric fuel pumps. Number 2 pump can empty the whole tank, but Number 1 pump cannot pump out the last three gallons, so that

LIST OF EXTRAS. Chronograph clock (fitted), **£7 7s.** Speedometer (mounted on bracket) **£5 6s.** The following are the special M.G. colours :—

Ulster Green/Dublin Green	Abingdon Grey/Brooklands Grey
Carmine Red/Saratoga Red	Light Fawn/Old Ivory
Oxford Blue/Cambridge Blue	Ebony Black/White

or Black exterior with a choice of leathers, as detailed below, and wheels cellulosed to match the upholstery.

Special colours other than the above, **£4 10s.**
Any deviation from any one of the five following standard leathers :—Apple Green, Tudor Brown, Deep Red, Cerulean Blue, Suede Grey leather, **£5 5s.**
Special back axle ratios other than standard range, **£15.**

PRICES.

Chassis. Supercharged, with straightforward gearbox	£550
Ditto with close ratio pre-selective gearbox	£575
Two-seater. T.T. type Coachwork, with straightforward gearbox	£625
Ditto with close ratio pre-selective gearbox	£650
Detachable streamlined tail for T.T. type body ...	£35
Two-seater. Streamlined model, with straightforward gearbox	£670
Ditto with close ratio pre-selective gearbox	£695
	ex Works

The right is reserved to vary this specification without notice.
Issued April, 1933—Reprinted May, 1933

SELECTED
BIBLIOGRAPHY

Allison, Mike, *The Magic of M.G.,* 1972

Autocar, *MG Sports*,* 1975

Blower, W. E., *The MG Workshop Manual,* 1952

Brooklands Reprints, *MG Cars in the 1930's; MG Cars 1929–1934; MG Cars 1935–1940; MG Cars 1940–1947; MG Cars 1948–1951; MG Cars 1952–1954; MG Cars 1955–1957; MG Cars 1957–1959*

Eyston, George, *Safety Last,* 1976; *Flat Out*,* 1933; *Flat Out (Second Edition),* 1976

Heygate, T., *Motor Tramp*,* 1935

Jacobs, Dick, *An MG Experience,* 1976

Knudson, Richard L., *The "T" Series MG,* 1974; *Classic MG Yearbook 1973,* 1974; *Classic MG Yearbook 1974,* 1975; *MG: The Sports Car America Loved First,* 1975

Knudson, Richard L., and Lavery, John M., *MG World/75,* 1976

Lyndon, Barre, *Combat*,* 1933; *Circuit Dust*,* 1934; *Grand Prix*,* 1935

May, C. A. N., *Wheelspin,* 1945;

McComb, F. Wilson, *The Story of the MG Sports Car*,* 1972

McKay, David, *Behind the Wheel*,* 1960

Thornley, John, *Maintaining the Breed,* 1950

Ullyett, Kenneth, *The MG Companion*,* 1960

Wherry, Joseph, *The MG Story*,* 1967

  * Out of print.

NOTE: We would be pleased to receive additions to this bibliography. Books with a distinct M.G. content should be suggested.

CREDITS

Allison, Mike (files) : 41, 42, 43

Bekker, John : 4, 5, 30, 31, 32, 33, 34, 35, 36, 37, 38, 39, 40

Boiteau, Betsey : 108 (bottom), 109 (top)

Boiteau, John : 111 (top)

Boiteau, John Jr.: 108 (top), 109 (bottom)

British Airways : 113 (top)

Cobban, Gordon (files) : 125, 126, 127, 128

Cover, Ron : 3, 22, 23, 25, 45, 80, 87, 88, 90

Ellman-Brown, Mike : 119, 120, 124

Ewing, Norman (files) : 100, 101, 102, 103, 104

Green, Malcolm : cover, 78, 86, 93

Griffiths, Guy : 44 (bottom), 46

Krook, Wiard : 106, 113 (bottom), 114, 115, 116, 117, 118

Leyland Historic Vehicles, Ltd : 8, 10, 12, 13, 14, 15, 16, 17, 18, 19, 20, 21, 26, 27, 76, 79, 80, 81, 82, 83, 84, 85, 86, 87, 89, 90, 91, 92, 93, 94, 95, 96, 97, 99, 133, 134, 142

Neal, Peter : the artwork in connection with "The Sign of the Octagon"

Seager, Stuart : 44 (top), 121, 122, 123

Stone, Henry (files) : 6, 9

Thornley, John (files) : 8 (top)

Wanklin, Earl : 7, 24, 92, 107, 108 (top), 110, 111 (bottom), 112

NOTE: "Milestone M.G.: The TC" is adapted from an earlier piece which appeared in *The Milestone Car,* Winter, 1975.